Ideology and the Future of Progressive Social Movements

Ideology and the Future of Progressive Social Movements

Rafal Soborski

ROWMAN &
LITTLEFIELD
——————INTERNATIONAL
London • New York

Published by Rowman & Littlefield International Ltd
Unit A, Whitacre Mews, 26–34 Stannary Street, London SE11 4AB
www.rowmaninternational.com

Rowman & Littlefield International Ltd.is an affiliate of Rowman & Littlefield
4501 Forbes Boulevard, Suite 200, Lanham, Maryland 20706, USA
With additional offices in Boulder, New York, Toronto (Canada), and Plymouth (UK)
www.rowman.com

British Library Cataloguing in Publication Data
A catalogue record for this book is available from the British Library

ISBN: HB 978-1-78348-792-9
           PB 978-1-78348-793-6

Library of Congress Cataloging-in-Publication Data Available

ISBN: 978-1-78348-792-9 (cloth)
ISBN: 978-1-78348-793-6 (pbk.)
ISBN: 978-1-78348-794-3 (electronic)

For Tomi, as always

Contents

Preface and Acknowledgements

A decade has passed since the financial crisis laid bare the destructive nature of neoliberal capitalism. Much ink has been spilled since then over the character and implications of social movements opposing the system, the reasons why it took them so long – roughly four years – to mobilize following the crisis and whether they have made any meaningful difference. However, while the literature on anti-neoliberal activism is already voluminous and continues to expand, the question of ideology's role in recent mobilizations is only beginning to be considered reflecting a broader, widely held belief that we now live in a post-ideological age. This book aims to fill this gap in existing scholarship. As the passage of time has allowed some analytical distance, and discursive material available for study has accumulated sufficiently, an exploration of the role that ideology plays in anti-neoliberal resistance is now warranted. While I share the discontent of the movements discussed here with shocking levels of inequality and blatant unfairness engendered by neoliberal practices, the discussion that follows may not come across as a sympathetic account. It is critical of the vague and moralistic way in which discontent has been expressed by anti-neoliberal movements, their preoccupation with themselves rather than the outside world and their substitution of ritualistic and theatrical forms of protest for concrete political agendas. In particular, the book demonstrates how the neglect of overt ideological work by anti-neoliberal activists has left the field open for cultivation by neoliberals as well as the far right. In contrast to much of the literature on anti-neoliberal activism, this book does not aim to celebrate its subject but rather, in the spirit of constructive critique, to highlight some of its limitations that should be addressed if anti-neoliberal movements are to take advantage of the next political opportunity. I leave it to the reader, of course, to judge if the book delivers what it sets out to do.

Before I begin, however, I would like to express my gratitude to several people without whose help and support this book would not have been possible. The research presented here started with a paper that I presented at the Political Economy of the World System Thirty-Eighth Annual Conference 'Social Movements and Global Transformation' which took place during 10–12 April 2014 at University of Pittsburgh. I am grateful to the organizers of the event for the enlightening discussions that we had in Pittsburgh and for inviting me to publish a chapter in the volume that followed (Smith et al. 2017; Soborski 2017). The transformation of the preliminary discussion in that chapter into this short book would not have happened without Anna Reeve who encouraged me to submit a proposal to Rowman & Littlefield International and, as Senior Commissioning Editor in Politics and International Relations, saw it through to acceptance. The proposal was reviewed by Michael Freeden and Jan Nederveen Pieterse, and I am indebted to both of them for their insightful feedback and detailed advice that greatly improved the quality of the discussion; all weaknesses that remain are, needless to say, of my own making. Much of the reading and research that underpins this book was done during the summer of 2016 at the Institute of European Studies at the Jagiellonian University in Krakow. I owe my sincere thanks to Dariusz Niedzwiedzki and Marcin Galent for hosting me there as a visiting researcher. The quiet and beautiful location of the institute helped me to focus my thoughts on the research, while the long and fascinating conversations I had with Marcin contributed greatly to sharpening my understanding of the central themes of this volume. Finally, I would also like to thank Dhara Patel and Rebecca Anastasi as well as the rest of the team at Rowman & Littlefield International for their invaluable assistance and patience with my requests: It was a great pleasure working with you on this project.

Chapter 1

Neoliberalism and Its Discontents in the Wake of the Crisis

This chapter sets out the book's argument by shedding some preliminary light on ideological struggles between neoliberalism and its challengers in the wake of the recent global financial crisis. The chapter offers a brief description of neoliberalism as ideology as well as discusses its initial fall from grace after the financial earthquake of 2007–2008 and its surprisingly quick recuperation soon afterwards. The reversely corresponding rise and decline of the latest wave of anti-neoliberal mobilization is also explored on the background of a broader introductory account of anti-neoliberal activism in the post–Cold War era. The chapter concludes with a concise preview of the main considerations advanced in this book.

THE CRUNCH

> Only a crisis – actual or perceived – produces real change. When that crisis occurs, the actions that are taken depend on the ideas that are lying around. (Friedman 2002, xiv)

The 2007–2008 financial collapse was the worst economic catastrophe since the Wall Street Crash of 1929. Estimates of the overall cost of the 'credit crunch' and the ensuing 'Great Recession' vary widely, but even the most conservative calculations are shocking. According to Bank of England Chief Economist Andrew Haldane (2010, 4), the output loss was between US\$60 trillion and US\$200 trillion for the world and between £1.8 trillion and £7.4 trillion for the United Kingdom. In the United States, the price tag has been estimated by some to come to a whopping US\$120,000 per person (Porter 2014). Behind these colossal figures lies incalculable misery of millions

1

of people who lost their homes, jobs and any sense of economic security that they had enjoyed. The recession was also exceptionally protracted, and any recovery has so far been pallid. The countries of the Global North are stuck in what seems like a permanent stagnation, and real living standards remain squeezed in even the strongest economies of the capitalist core; real wages in Britain, for example, declined by more than 10 percent between 2007 and 2015 (Allen and Elliott 2016). At the same time, peripheries of the core, especially countries in southern Europe, are still in a profound crisis whose depth is epitomized by the situation in Greece where incomes of the poorest fifth of the population have fallen by 42 percent since 2009 and in 2016 unemployment rate was a staggering 24 percent while the value of the national debt was almost twice the value of the country's economy (Smith 2016). Admittedly, the crisis has damaged the economies of the broadly defined Global North more, by and large, than those of Global East and South, and so can be seen as an element of a 'global rebalancing', particularly between the Atlantic core and South East Asia (Nederveen Pieterse 2011). That said, the slowdown has impeded the growth of even the most dynamic, newly industrialized countries, while its impact on sub-Saharan Africa is proving particularly detrimental (Dolphin and Chappell 2010; UNCTAD 2016).

The worst economic downturn since the 1930s was caused by rampant deregulation of financial markets driven by the agenda of the 'free market' ideology known as neoliberalism. This assertion is not controversial: It is not only the view from any perspective to the left of free market fundamentalism, but it is also the finding of the two most important US government investigations into the crisis (Levin and Coburn 2011; The Financial Crisis Inquiry Commission 2011). The policies of liberalization, financialization and deregulation leading to the crash were relentlessly legitimized, promoted and implemented by preachers of the free-market doctrine. The culpability of neoliberalism became apparent, although only in retrospect, even to those who had been in charge of the global financial system prior to the collapse (at least before the majority of them embarked on the project of neoliberal reconsolidation and hence vigorously denied any connection between laissez-faire and the meltdown). A highly symbolic case in point is the response by the neoliberal 'oracle', Alan Greenspan, to grilling from the House Committee on Oversight and Government Reform in October 2008. Greenspan found himself forced to admit that there was 'a flaw' in the free-market doctrine that he had worked so zealously to put into practice since first appointed Federal Reserve Chairman by President Reagan in August 1987 (Andrews 2008).

The harm caused by the crunch is of extraordinary magnitude, but it was far from the only crisis of the post–Cold War neoliberal era. The 1997 financial catastrophe in South East Asia, which impacted particularly badly on Thailand, Indonesia, South Korea and the Philippines and then reverberated in Russia and Brazil in 1998, the 2001 dot.com bubble burst and the Argentinean crisis that began in the same year are just some of the other major disasters that can be traced straight back to practices of speculation and financialization. What is more, while it is prone to recurring convulsions, neoliberal capitalism failed to deliver genuine economic growth even in its ostensibly good times (Harvey 2006, 33; Birch and Mykhnenko 2010). In fact, the average growth rate in the more economically developed 'Western' economies during capitalism's Keynesian era was double of what neoliberal capitalism achieved there from the 1980s onwards (Jacques 2016). Furthermore, in Marxist terms, 'neoliberalism has not proven effective at revitalizing global capital accumulation, but it has succeeded in restoring class power' (Harvey 2006, 29). It has done this by facilitating the transfer of unprecedented quantities of wealth upwards to the already super-rich. The resulting dramatic increase in inequality has been extensively documented (Milanovic 2016; Piketty 2014), and its scale has been such that at one point even the notorious International Monetary Fund (IMF) made a volte-face away from its typically neoliberal position concerning the impact of the growing gap between the rich and the poor and the policies to mitigate it (Ostry, Loungani and Furceri 2016).

According to a long-established tradition of radical critique (e.g., Polanyi 2001 [1944]), as long as neoliberalism remains dominant, its continued push towards a free-market dystopia will carry on destroying the planet, eroding social cohesion and suppressing individual life chances except for the privileged few. Yet, at the same time, neoliberalism's opponents have a lot to learn from the way their adversary gained the ground in the past four decades. This point was previously made by others (Anderson 2000; Srnicek and Williams 2015) and will be reiterated throughout the book, but it is useful to note at the outset some of the key moments in the extraordinary career of neoliberalism as a system of economic and political beliefs and prescriptions – in short, as ideology.[1]

THE VILLAIN

To allow the market mechanism to be sole director of the fate of human beings and their natural environment . . . would result in the demolition of society. . . . Robbed of the protective covering of cultural institutions, human beings would perish from the effects of social exposure; they would die as the victims of acute social dislocation through vice, perversion, crime, and starvation. Nature would be reduced to its elements, neighborhoods and landscapes defiled, rivers polluted, military safety jeopardized, the power to produce food and raw materials destroyed. (Polanyi 2001 [1944], 76)

Neoliberal ideology has its origins in classical liberal economics, especially of Ricardian ilk, and displays a striking similarity to the market-zealous argumentation advanced by so-called Manchesterism, a loose name for economic and political movements for trade liberalization in England, particularly in the 1840s (Soborski 2009 and 2013, 43–71). Neoliberal socio-political prescriptions overlap also with late-nineteenth century Social Darwinist justification of competition between individuals as the law of nature. More recent influences include the laissez-faire doctrine of 'objectivism' associated with Ayn Rand. As a distinctive ideological current, neoliberalism is usually traced back to the establishment, primarily thanks to the efforts of the Austrian economist Friedrich Hayek, of the Mont Pèlerin Society, an international organization of 'free-market' enthusiasts named after the Swiss resort where it was first convened in 1947. Hayek's winning of the Nobel Prize in economics in 1974, ending years of his academic marginalization and coinciding with an escalation of contradictions within capitalism's Keynesian model, is a symbolic marker of the beginning of neoliberalism's astounding rise to global hegemony.

Hayek's Nobel Prize was followed by the imposition of neoliberal policies in Chile under the dictatorship of General Augusto Pinochet and electoral victories of two politicians in whom Hayek found charismatic popularizers and very effective enactors of his economic doctrine: Margaret Thatcher in 1979 in Britain and Ronald Reagan in 1980 in the United States. The subsequent erosion of social democracy and the mixed economy across the capitalist world, the transformation of China's socio-economic system from Maoism into 'neoliberalism with Chinese characteristics' (Harvey 2007, 120–52) and the collapse of the Soviet bloc with the subsequent 'shock therapy' of marketization and liberalization in countries like Russia and Poland (Klein 2007) complete neoliberalism's expansion to almost every corner of the planet.

Inevitably for a truly global system of beliefs and practices, neoliberalism has had numerous distinct local expressions. Indeed, like any socio-economic doctrine, neoliberalism is never 'pure' but always in the process of mutating into hybrid forms depending on specific temporal and spatial contexts (Kingfisher 2007; Leitner, Peck and Sheppard 2007; Ward and England 2007, 255). Likewise, the depth of its hegemony continues to vary. The Anglo-American world, the birthplace and cradle of economic liberalism, seems to have been penetrated more thoroughly than other regions. On the other hand, more or less effective push-backs against neoliberalism occurred in recent decades in parts of Latin America, triggered by a mixture of colonial legacy, current geopolitical factors and an entrenched tradition of left-wing populist politics in the region (Dello Buono and Bell Lara 2007; Sader 2008).

The diversity of settings in which neoliberalism operates and the resulting variety of its discursive articulations and policy outcomes need to be acknowledged. However, to enhance the flow of this book's argument, I will tend to speak of neoliberalism in singular, or of 'neoliberalism-in-general' (Peck 2004, 403), an ideal type (Coser 1977, 223–24) constructed on the basis of family resemblances (Gaus 2000, 19) between different situated instances of the ideology with all their contradictions, meanderings and also backtrackings that some analysts prefer to call 'neoliberalizations' (England and Ward 2007). I will thus rely on a rather broad definition of neoliberalism, as exemplified by Jamie Peck's and Adam Tickell's description: 'a distinctive political economic philosophy that took meaningful shape for the first time during the 1970s, dedicated to the extension of market (and market-like) forms of governance, rule, and control across – tendentially at least – all spheres of social life' (Peck and Tickell 2007, 28).

If neoliberalism serves the interests of only a tiny group of the super-wealthy and periodically wreaks havoc on the global economy, not to mention its disastrous implications for the natural environment (Monbiot 2014), then the question is why it has risen, so relentlessly, to a position of global hegemony, economically, politically and institutionally, and why it remains, with few exceptions, by and large the only game in town, even after neoliberal practices caused one of the deepest economic recessions the world has ever known. Before the 2007–2008 turmoil, the hegemonic status of neoliberalism was certainly not in doubt: Indeed, it was widely perceived as 'the most successful ideology in world history' (Anderson 2000, 17). Its ideas dictated economic and social policies worldwide and spilled all over the ideological spectrum, making deep inroads into other political traditions including social democracy, where the so called Third Way, put forward by Anthony Giddens (2008) and associated particularly with Tony Blair and Bill Clinton, turned out to be a very faithful adaptation. But even now, in spite of the enormous costs of neoliberalism's most recent excesses, its position seems unshakable. This is not to deny that neoliberalism's status may not be quite like the one it enjoyed before. William Davis (2016) has a point when he argues that the current incarnation of neoliberalism differs from its pre-crisis triumphant antecedent. According to Davis, this is, in fact, a 'post-hegemonic' neoliberalism, one 'without normative or democratic authority' (123) and based instead 'around an ethos of punishment' (124) associated with austerity. But Davis may have 'exaggerated the importance of the popular "consent" function of the hegemonic ideology' (Desai 1994, 38), and so his argument as to the post-hegemony situation of neoliberalism may be premature. Using a different turn of phrase, Neil Smith (2010, 56) describes the present-day condition of neoliberalism as 'dead yet still dominant'. While the characterization of neoliberal hegemony as zombie-like is captivating – and has for some time been trending in post-crisis accounts of neoliberalism (e.g., Peck 2014; Wright 2015, 111) – this does not alter the fact that its grip on people's lives all over the world continues to be very tight and real. After all, as Colin Leys (1990, 127) remarked, 'for an ideology to be hegemonic, it is not necessary that it be loved. It is merely necessary that it have no serious rival'.

The enduring power of neoliberalism, whatever the degree of its legitimacy in the eyes of the public, is not what was generally anticipated amid the turbulences of 2007–2008. In fact, the initial outburst of the crisis and its immediate aftermath signalled to many, not just on the political left, an inexorable decline of neoliberal supremacy and a unique political opening for its opponents. It was, or so it appeared, a difficult time for 'free-market' advocates. As I have already noted, key protagonists of the foregoing orthodoxy, even highly influential figures like Alan Greenspan, were forced to withdraw to more defensive positions, and the initial reaction of the majority of governments in the Global North, most of them resolutely neoliberal in policy and outlook until that time, was to turn towards interventionism to an extent unprecedented in the decades before the crunch. At that early stage the series of enormous bailouts indicated a possibility of a major Keynesian shift in economic policy. This was reinforced by political declarations coming from the very top, including the most unlikely voices. Thus, the right-wing President of France, Nicolas Sarkozy, all of a sudden spoke as a convert to social democracy: 'The idea of the absolute power of the markets that should not be constrained by any rule, by any political intervention, was a mad idea. The idea that markets are always right was a mad idea' (Samuel 2008). The 2009 Inaugural Address by President Barack Obama (2009a) stroke a similarly Keynesian note: '[the market's] power to generate wealth and expand freedom is unmatched. But this crisis has reminded us that without a watchful eye, the market can spin out of control'. Bold statements were made by many other state leaders, but the British Prime Minister at the time, Gordon Brown, articulated the commonplace of that (brief) time in a particularly evocative way: 'The old world of the Washington Consensus is over' (in Steger and Roy 2010, 133).

Yet, what then seemed like a genuinely Keynesian shift was nothing of the sort. While the aftermath of the 2007–2008 financial upheaval did look as though a time of opportunity for (more) progressive politics had finally arrived, with the benefit of hindsight it soon became obvious that the statist intervention in response to the credit crunch consisted in the socialization of banks' losses and that subsequent policy measures were archetypically neoliberal in nature. At the same time, the initial consternation among neoliberal elites soon gave way to policy and discursive reconsolidation. The banking crisis was redefined as the sovereign debt crisis, and the policies of deregulation, privatization and rolling back of the welfare state have continued, with even greater vigour, often accompanied by the conservative rhetoric of the 'Big Society', essentially a Victorian vision of the voluntary sector taking over most of the social functions of the state and hence supposedly mitigating the impact of austerity.

The reasons for this surprisingly quick recovery of neoliberalism have been discussed at length. Commentators note that while the doctrine may have suffered intellectually, the material circumstances and social, particularly class, structures underlying the supremacy of neoliberal practices have not been removed; in other words, 'the illusions have survived the bonfire', because they are 'illusions sustained by material interests' (Callinicos 2010, x; see also: Crouch 2011, viii and 1; Gamble 2009, 89–90; Nederveen Pieterse 2011 and 2012, 14–15; Radice 2011, 139). Accordingly, just as the entrenched interests have not been dislodged, so likewise the arguments and narratives that defend them have remained in place. But while material and structural factors underlying 'the strange non-death of neoliberalism' (Crouch 2011) are certainly not to be ignored, a further key reason for the resurgence of neoliberalism has been its skilful remobilization of political ideas and its steady, continued and voluminous ideological output. This is not to suggest that it is only ideology that matters: ideological developments are, of course, supported by material structures. However, importantly, the opposite is also true: 'Material incentives and policies have *ideological* conditions of existence' (Leys 1990, 126, emphasis in original).

Almost immediately after the financial calamity, laissez-faire intellectuals and think tanks – the Adam Smith Institute, Institute of Economic Affairs, Cato Institute, Heritage Foundation and many others – initiated the neoliberal counter-offensive in the form of many arguments, rebuttals and rejoinders advancing the neoliberal case post the credit crunch. Their discourse has been quite uniform in its persistent reiterating of the free-market dogma. Eamonn Butler (2008), Director of Adam Smith Institute, thus blamed political institutions for the global economic convulsion and reaffirmed the virtues of markets: 'Western capitalism has been dealt a severe blow by inept politicians and officials. But global capitalism continues to pull hundreds of millions of people out of poverty. It's a great system. Let's not break it'. Tom Clougherty (2009), representing the same think tank, likewise called free marketeers to oppose the 'Keynesian revival': 'Markets need defending, and we are the people to do it. . . . It is also important that we continue to make the case that it was not unbridled free markets, but rather interventionist governments which caused the 2008 crisis'. Other contributors to the institute's publishing output concurred, 'Public agents, not private ones . . . are to blame for the crisis' (Lal 2009); 'every investor and gold bug should know the enemy: Keynes, the advocate of big government and the welfare state, and Karl Marx' (Skousen 2009); 'market economy is the only way' (Lundberg 2012). Commentators at the Institute of Economic Affairs were

as unequivocal, blaming 'governments, not markets' (Butler 2009) and call-
ing for 'minimal regulation, or even no regulation at all' (Beenstock 2009,
59). Some also added a distinctly conservative twist to this argumentation –
accordingly, what markets both require and reward is traditional morality:
'No amount of regulation – heavy or light – can substitute for the type of
character formation that is supposed to occur in families, schools, churches
and synagogues' (Gregg 2009, 151). The list of examples could go on – the
blogosphere quickly became saturated with myriad claims advancing the
neoliberal case post the credit crunch. Such highly ideologically charged
accounts have been consistent and unequivocal in reiterating the free-market
dogma and have made a very important contribution towards the latest reas-
sertion of neoliberal policies across the world.

THE CONTESTANTS

> Leftists assume that our lack of good political ideas means the end of
> politics as such. If the game isn't played on our terms, we aren't going to
> play at all. We aren't even going to recognize that a game is being played.
> (Dean 2009, 12)

While neoliberalism appears to be if not alive and kicking then at least
enduring, its opponents have struggled to sustain momentum, ironically at
a time that would seem particularly receptive to their critique. A range of
explanations have been provided to account for this unimpressive record of
counter-hegemonic politics. Unwillingness to commit to a policy programme,
enact an effective political strategy, and, in particular, work towards influencing or capturing the institutions of the state have all been noted as key
problems by left-wing commentators with different emphases depending on
their specific ideological location on the socialist continuum (Boggs 2012;
Brass 2014; Pugh 2011; Žižek 2013). As I will discuss in later chapters,
an animated debate ensued between the critics and the defenders of anti-
neoliberal movements' preoccupation with counter-cultural spontaneity
and their refusal of firm strategies (e.g., Callinicos and Holloway 2011).
But again, although arguments highlighting weaknesses in political strategy
have strong grounds, there is a more deep-seated source of disorientation
among movements contesting neoliberalism and, just as with the success
of neoliberalism, it can be found in the ideational sphere. The problem
lies in how these movements, and fellow-travelling intellectuals, tend to
approach the role of ideology in political action. The ideological dimension is a fundamental one to consider when explaining the track record of
progressive anti-neoliberal politics because it is ideology that underpins

political programmes and informs policy solutions. Accepting this point, which I will substantiate in chapter 2, reveals the problematic nature of some popular perceptions, unwittingly parroted by progressives after neoliberals, of ideology's present-day condition and application.

It is important to note that what is often described, both by activists and by commentators, as *the* movement against neoliberalism is in reality an extremely heterogeneous plethora of various mobilizations, struggles and discourses, articulated either in terms of opposition to neoliberalism as a whole or as contestations of some aspects and implications of neoliberal praxis, including obscene global and national inequality, austerity, war or environmental degradation. The challengers of neoliberalism belong, knowingly or not, to different ideological traditions – on the right, including traditional conservatism, national populism and fascism (Soborski 2013, 107–39), as well as the left. This book is focused on *progressive* anti-neoliberal positions, namely, contestations of neoliberalism on behalf of egalitarian goals associated with the left. Of course, this is still a highly general delineation, and more fine-grained distinctions are usually needed to highlight the different perspectives – Marxist, anarchist and so on – from which the progressive challengers of neoliberalism advance their respective arguments. In any case, the discussion presented in this book does not cover right-wing positions whose anti-neoliberalism is motivated by the wish to advance the interests of a particular social stratum (usually an ethnic group or religious community), in sharp contrast with their neglect or active vilification of other groups (e.g., immigrants or ethnic minorities).[2]

Specific articulations of progressive resistance to neoliberalism depend on given socio-economic circumstances and ideological contexts: while in the Global North, anarchist and social-democratic models seem particularly relevant (albeit not often explicitly acknowledged), in the Global South and East (post-)colonialism is probably the most important conceptual background for anti-neoliberal arguments and narratives. Forms of political activism vary as much as discourses that motivate them and, again, depend on time and place. Furthermore, the term *neoliberalism* is not universally used to capture the object of the movements' critique and contestation: for example, it is a much more likely descriptor in the European context than in North America (Peck 2010, 2). As Helga Leitner et al. (2007, 13–14) note, 'Neoliberalism may also be contested when it is not conceived as the principal culprit. The principal target of contestation may be some other source of oppression or injustice, but neoliberalism may still be contested when it is perceived as facilitating these other injustices'. Thus, in the Global South, many political struggles against neoliberalism have been articulated primarily as protests against its institutional embodiments, especially the World Bank and the IMF, and their policies of 'structural adjustment' (Balanyá et al. 2005). In turn, a related focus on fiscal austerity and cuts to public services has been particularly pre-dominant in Europe after 2008. Many other social struggles – for example, against 'corporate' capitalism, against 'globalization', against privatization of public space and so on – can all be included under the broad umbrella of anti-neoliberalism even when their conceptual lexicons do not highlight the term itself.

The latest wave of anti-neoliberal campaigns is a manifestation of a series of social struggles with a long and kaleidoscopic history. While this book is concerned primarily with the most recent mobilizations, it brings into dis-cussion also some examples from the 1990s and early 2000s in the Global North. The rationale behind this regional focus is an especial persistence in the activist repertoires in the wealthy parts of the world of problems and flaws that have seriously limited the effectiveness of anti-neoliberal move-ments there. Although the book draws mainly on the latest developments and their immediate predecessors, some contextualization relating to earlier influences, for example, the New Left, will also be provided as opposition to neoliberalism can be traced back to the 1970s, the decade when neoliberalism itself 'took off'.

Early eruptions of discontent with neoliberal policies include the 1977 Egyptian 'Bread Riots' (McMahon 2017, 173) and the 1989 insurgence in Venezuela (López Maya 2003). Later, worldwide attention focused in particular on the Zapatista uprising in Chiapas, Mexico, that began in 1994 following the North American Free Trade Agreement which posed a threat to the livelihoods of the indigenous population (Khasnabish 2010). The so-called 'Cochabamba Water War' against privatization in Bolivia in 1999–2000 (Olivera 2004) and the 2001 uprising in Argentina (Libcom 2005) are other examples of anti-neoliberal struggles in the South. There have also been numerous direct action campaigns against neoliberalism in cities in the Global South as well as North (Bond and McInnes 2007; Oldfield and Stokke 2007). As for the, already mentioned, 1990s' 'anti-globalization movement' in the Global North (or, more correctly, 'alter-globalization', as most of its constituent groups and campaigns were unequivocally cosmopolitan in outlook), international attention was drawn in particular to the succession of protests – in Seattle (1999), Prague (2000), Genoa (2001) and elsewhere – which assembled a huge diversity of groups, from trade unions to feminist, anarchist and ecologist movements (for early overviews, see Ayres 2004; Glassman 2001; Kingsnorth 2003; Mertes 2004; Notes from Nowhere 2003; Starr 2000, 2005). World Social Forums, beginning with the 2001 Forum in Porto Alegre, Brazil, and their regional equivalents have attracted a lot of interest as well. Coinciding with the elite World Economic Forums in Davos, the Social Forums are gatherings of diverse non-governmental organizations and social movements critical of neoliberalism. They provide an opportunity for activists to express their discontent with the globalization of free-market capitalism and discuss alternatives to it (Santos 2006; Sen and Waterman 2009; Smith et al. 2016).

Previewing the argument that follows in subsequent chapters, the alter-globalist or 'global justice' movement (to reiterate, both are umbrella terms for a plethora of different groups, campaigns and mobilizations in the 1990s and early 2000s) disappointed many sympathetic commentators and foreshadowed many of the limitations of the most recent wave of anti-neoliberal resistance (Gilbert 2008; Srnicek and Williams 2015; Toynbee 2009). Like other instances of post-1960s' 'new radicalism', alter-globalism tended to remain, in the words of Carl Boggs (2012, 14), 'local, dispersed, and pre-political' and 'never generated durable (organizational and ideological) alternatives to entrenched power structures'. Pitfalls of the global justice movement are discussed in several parts of this book as they provide a useful background for its main argument about the most recent wave of anti-neoliberal activism that erupted after the financial collapse.[3]

Fast forward to that latest wave of anti-neoliberal discontent, the political protests following the crisis did not begin immediately; they took some time to heat. Mervyn King, Bank of England's Governor at that time, actually expressed his (positive) surprise that there had been little public anger visible in the aftermath of the crunch and the subsequent huge taxpayer-funded bailouts for the perpetrators (*The Telegraph* 2011). While there had been some local protests, notably in Greece (from December 2008 onwards) and Iceland (the 'Pots and Pans Revolution' climaxing in early 2009), global political unrest did not erupt until late 2010. Its explosion is symbolically marked by the self-immolation of a street vendor, Mohamed Bouazizi, in the Tunisian town of Sidi Bouzid. Bouazizi had been harassed by the police for many years – when unable to pay them a bribe, he had his wares confiscated as well as suffering regular humiliation at their hands – his suicide followed one of such incidents. He immediately became a martyr of the anti-government protests that had been triggered by his death and quickly spread across Tunisia leading to President Ben Ali fleeing the country and the establishment of a democratic government. The events in Tunisia prompted a wave of riots across North Africa and in countries of the Persian Gulf. This was quickly dubbed the 'Arab Spring' as Libya, Egypt, Yemen, Syria and Iraq were particularly affected. While this was a rebellion against political authoritarianism, it was also underpinned by people's anger at extreme levels of inequality in the region and economic decline exacerbated by neoliberal crisis (Dabashi 2012).

The Arab Spring, and particularly the uprising in Egypt, has been studied extensively by social movements scholars. Special attention has been paid to the role of social networking platforms, such as Facebook and Twitter, in organizing the protests (see, e.g., Gerbaudo 2012, 48–75). Claims that these were 'Twitter' or 'Facebook' revolutions (Cohen 2011) and 'not possible without Mark Zuckerberg' (Webster 2011) will be critically assessed in chapter 3. It should be noted that the fate of the Arab Spring – the fact that it was soon followed by what some dubbed the 'Arab Winter' (*The Washington Times* 2011) – was determined by factors that are not encountered by anti-austerity campaigns in liberal-democratic states of the Western world. However, the effectiveness of recent struggles in Arab countries has also, like in Europe or North America, been limited by a lack of ideological orientation and organizational strategy (Badiou 2012, 42; Bayat 2013). This is, of course, just one, albeit important, reason why, aside perhaps from the Tunisian case, the revolutions did not bring about political democratization let alone greater equality. Such hopes were quashed quickly by counter-revolutions in Egypt, foreign interventions in Bahrain and Yemen and the eruption of civil wars in Syria and Libya.

Europe's southern countries were the venue of the next major escalation of dissatisfaction with rising poverty levels and the yawning gap between the haves and the have-nots. In March 2011, the Portuguese movement against austerity known as *Geração à Rasca* ('Desperate Generation') organized the largest demonstrations since the country's 1974 Carnation Revolution. These actions then influenced the 15-M movement in Spain that began with the encampment of the Puerta del Sol square in Madrid on 15 May 2011 but had its roots in *Democracia Real YA* ('Real Democracy NOW') and *Juventud Sin Futuro* ('Youth Without a Future') networks. The movement protested against high unemployment (more than 20% overall at the time, but 40% among young people), welfare cuts and neoliberal restructuring of the country. The Iberian protests made their mark on street activism in Greece and other European states, as well as the Israeli anti-neoliberal mobilization in August 2011 (Rosenhek and Shalev 2013) and the 'Gezi protests' in Istanbul, Turkey, in May 2013 (Çiğdem 2017). This broad international movement, known as *Indignados* ('the Indignants'), received extensive attention from commentators and scholars. However, in spite of its quickly attained publicity and mass character – it is estimated that up to 8 million Spaniards participated in its various events at some point (Carty 2015, 130) – the movement seems to be largely dormant at present, and the question is whether its aversion towards formal political structures and explicit programmes has prevented it from having a lasting effect (Badiou 2012, 97–99; Winlow et al. 2015, 169–84; Žižek 2011). The discourse of the *Indignados* is characterized by an anti-institutional emphasis on prefigurative politics and disinclination to offer practical solutions – problems that will be discussed in chapter 4.

The *Indignados* share several characteristics, including the aforementioned limitations, with the mobilization symbolizing the climax of anti-neoliberal struggles post the 2007–2008 crisis in the Global North. This came in September 2011 when the activist occupation of the Zuccotti Park in Manhattan began triggering a wave of occupations that spread, by mid-October, to 900 cities all over the world (Adam 2011). The Occupy movement was brought together by the '99 percent' slogan that centred the movement's narrative on the extremes of wealth amassed by the top 1 percent of the population. While subject of numerous studies and cause of great hope to many progressives (Hardt and Negri 2012; Van Gelder 2011) the Occupy movement was also short-lived. The occupation of Wall Street came to an abrupt end in mid-November when the police in riot gear forced the activists to leave. Elsewhere, occupations ended in the course of 2012. As I will show, particularly in chapters 4 and 5, the appeal of the movement – the lived experience of occupation and the sense of empowerment that it conferred on the participants as well as the captivating nature of its main narrative – was also its undoing. While the Occupy movement certainly exerted a significant biographical impact on its participants (Vestergren, Drury and Chiriac 2017) and also had some later valuable offshoots (Welty 2014), most commentators, including the movement's sympathizers, now look back at it with a sense of frustration due to its lack of political articulation, structure and strategy (Boggs 2012; Harris 2012; Hickel 2012; Srnicek and Williams 2015; Winlow et al. 2015; Žižek 2011).

All in all, the wave of protests after the 2007–2008 financial earthquake has not changed how capitalism operates let alone provided any real challenge to the continuation of the system. Neoliberal ideology and practice remain, for now at least, undefeated. At the same time, political space is increasingly occupied by more and more assertive right-wing agendas, a process in which the left has been complicit, albeit unwittingly, by not making a sufficient effort to construct compelling visions and narratives of its own (Grande 2013, 375–76; Winlow et al. 2015, 105–33). Donald Trump's win in the 2016 US elections and the preceding result of the Brexit referendum in the United Kingdom, the latter caused primarily by xenophobic fears reinforced by tabloid scaremongering about immigration, spring to mind as probably the most consequential examples of the trend.[4] It is in the context of the ongoing marginalization of progressive alternatives to neoliberalism that it becomes vital to reflect upon the reasons for the disappointing track record of anti-neoliberal activism at what was a time of unprecedented opportunity. While the literature on anti-neoliberalism is extensive and increasingly preoccupied with explaining its limitations, only a small number of scholarly accounts focus explicitly on ideology (exceptions are Lindholm and Zúquete 2010; Rupert 2000; Schwarzmantel 2008; Steger, Goodman and Wilson 2013) and even fewer employ the concept of ideology in a thorough, consistent and systematic way. This is the gap that this book seeks to fill.

CHAPTER CONTENT

Chapter 2 begins by shedding light at the concept of ideology, its substance and its functions, and then reviews the arguments to the effect that ideology has ended. The focus is first on conservative and liberal pronouncements of ideology's death as they help to contextualize the premises and problems of the widespread dismissal of ideology in the political communication of anti-neoliberal activists and intellectuals. The chapter then provides a preliminary account of how such claims were articulated within the global justice movement of the 1990s and the early 2000s as well as in connection with the more recent anti-austerity activism exemplified by the *Indignados* and Occupy movements. The chapter's core argument is that while the mainstream notion of the end of ideology has helped to buttress the hegemony of neoliberalism, its adoption by anti-neoliberal discourses has weakened their political impact.

Chapter 3 focuses on arguments highlighting, and typically celebrating, the networked forms of organization that epitomize contemporary transnational activism. The flexibility and decentralization of anti-neoliberal movements have been touted by activists and fellow-travelling intellectuals as reflecting the nature of the networking media that the activists rely on and, at the same time, as principles which render ideological differences within and between movements irrelevant. However, even though the idea of networking has an obvious relevance and appeal in a digital age, some of the associated naïve discourses of technology may have led the activists astray. The chapter provides a critical review of debates about the impact of the preoccupation with networks on political strategies, knowledge production and power mechanisms within both the global justice movement and the post-crisis anti-austerity activism.

In chapter 4, I am concerned with prefigurative politics, another key theme in the literature of and about radical activism today, and its prioritization of processes and principles of action – in particular, horizontality – over political goals. I demonstrate that emphasis on prefiguration tends to replace debates about political vision or policy measures with squabbles about the everyday logistics of activism. Furthermore, prefigurative politics has a highly individualistic dimension and, as such, is fairly compatible with some aspects of the neoliberal vision of human nature, especially its stress on autonomy and creativity. These and similar problems are discussed alongside associated claims about the irrelevance of ideology that have been put forward, sometimes in fairly unequivocal ways, by advocates of prefiguration.

While networking and prefiguration describe the movement's operative principles, the 99 percent catchphrase was supposed to encapsulate what the most recent expression of anti-neoliberal activism, and particularly the

Occupy movement, stood for. Chapter 5 covers a number of activist interpretations of the 99 percent idiom, examines its ideational genealogy and,
drawing on a range of scholarly contributions, sheds light on its repercussions, in particular, a tendency to avoid engaging with more thorny political
dilemmas. The disposition of the 99 percent discourse is populist, and so the
chapter engages with a number of leading evaluations of the character of, and
prospects for, a progressive form of populism. Some of the flaws of progressive populism's recent articulations are examined alongside a tentative consideration of what is needed to reclaim its mobilizing potential in the future.

The final chapter (chapter 6) draws together the main themes of this book
and reiterates the key point that I make throughout it, namely that anti-
neoliberal activists need to start treating ideas as a valuable political resource
that should be debated and cultivated. However, developing a powerful ideological narrative for today's politics of resistance will not be straightforward
due, among other challenges, to the multiplicity of perspectives that anti-
neoliberalism comprises. While a blueprint to address this and other
dilemmas discussed on the following pages would perhaps make for a nice
conclusion to my argument, this book is not intended as a piece of advocacy
or a normative manifesto. Therefore, the concluding chapter limits its ambi-
tions to a tentative consideration of merely some broad and open-ended
parameters of an ideology that would be compatible with the diversity and
dynamism of anti-neoliberal movements while also providing a firm foundation for counter-hegemonic politics.

NOTES

1. There is now a vast literature on multiple other aspects of neoliberalism:
An introductory account by Harvey (2007) provides a good summary of the principles and history of neoliberalism, while the *Routledge Handbook of Neoliberalism* (Springer, Birch and McLeavy 2016) offers a wide-ranging review of the main
debates concerning manifold implications of neoliberal theory and practice.

2. Far right responses to neoliberal globalization are discussed in my previous
book (Soborski 2013, 107–39).

3. Comparisons between the two waves of activism are common in insider (or
sympathetic) accounts of anti-neoliberal politics (see, e.g., della Porta 2012; Graeber
2011; Klein 2011; Maeckelbergh 2012; Smith 2012).

4. While the advances of the national populist right are, in and of themselves,
of grave concern to progressives, they have also proven perfectly compatible with
corporate priorities and have been used to intensify the neoliberal assault on society
(Klein 2017).

Chapter 2

Ideology and Its
Unwarranted Obituaries

This chapter begins by explaining the neutral conceptualization of political ideology which forms the basis of this book's argument. From the neutral perspective, ideologies are political belief systems providing individuals and groups with cognitive frameworks that mould their feelings, opinions and actions concerning existing socio-political arrangements as well as their visions of an ideal polity. While the neutral understanding of ideology prevails in mainstream political science, in real-life political discourse ideology remains if not a dirty word then at least a term with disparaging connotations. The chapter sheds a critical light on the evolution of negative meanings of ideology, examines the associated end of ideology debate and accentuates the very different implications of present-day pronouncements of ideology's death for neoliberalism and its opponents.

THE CONCEPT

> Those who are in ideology, you and I, believe that they are by definition outside ideology: one of the effects of ideology is the practical *denegation* of the ideological character of ideology by ideology: ideology never says, 'I am ideological'. (Althusser 2014 [1971], 191, emphasis in original)

The term 'ideology' was coined by Count Antoine Destutt de Tracy in his *Éléments d'Idéologie* (1804) to describe the academic discipline devoted to the study of ideas. Assuming, in a proto-positivist way, that all aspects of human consciousness have their roots in our senses, the French aristocrat described his own work as a branch of zoology though he also believed it to be crucial in designing and implementing a rational social order. De Tracy's scholarly investigation was initially supported by Napoleon Bonaparte, but eventually the liberal philosopher fell out of the emperor's favour. Napoleon turned against the entire school of *ideologues* led by de Tracy; he now chose to use 'ideology' as a word of abuse to describe 'shadowy metaphysics' (Thompson 1990, 31), an abstract and impractical domain of cerebral speculation. Napoleon's disparaging view of ideology was to have a considerable impact on the subsequent trajectories of the concept.

Contrary to negative understandings of ideology, initiated by Napoleon and discussed later in this chapter, the predominant academic tradition of ideology studies is neutral and inclusive in that it incorporates in the category of ideology all political belief systems, left or right wing, demanding change, whether revolutionary or gradual, or wishing to conserve the existing society, favoured by or abhorrent to the theorist undertaking their examination. This approach gives rise to the kind of definition that can be found in popular introductions to ideology studies:

> Ideology is a more or less coherent set of ideas that provides the basis for organized political action, whether this is intended to preserve, modify or overthrow the existing system of power. All ideologies therefore have the following features. They:
>
> (a) offer an account of the existing order, usually in the form of a 'world-view'
> (b) advance a model of a desired future, a vision of the 'good society'
> (c) explain how political change can and should be brought about – how to get from (a) to (b). (Heywood 2017, 10)

Or:

> A political ideology is a set of ideas, beliefs, opinions, and values that
>
> (1) exhibit a recurring pattern
> (2) are held by significant groups
> (3) compete over providing and controlling plans for public policy
> (4) do so with the aim of justifying, contesting or changing the social and political arrangements and processes of a political community. (Freeden 2003, 32)

While the first definition draws attention to discursive components of ideology, the second also highlights the contested nature of ideological discourse. Both definitions underscore the fact that ideology straddles the spheres of political thought and political action.

The neutral understanding of ideology, exemplified in these definitions, is the one on which I will rely in this book. Accordingly, *an* ideology is a particular political belief system such as liberalism, socialism or fascism, whereas ideology as a generic noun covers the characteristics common to all political belief systems; any such system is considered to be an ideology. While this approach may lead to epistemological relativism – because, at least for methodological purposes, it treats all ideologies, for example, Nazism as well as social democracy, as specimens of the same category – its benefits outweigh its shortcomings. Among its other advantages, the neutral conceptualization is conducive to the comparative study of political thought because it does not 'privilege' any political belief system as being of a different order, somehow 'above' ideology.

There are, broadly speaking, three analytical foci within the discipline of ideology studies: semantic, historical and functional. The semantic examination focuses on the meanings conveyed by any ideological system, on its explicit and implicit connotations and also its internal ideational tensions and contradictions. Semantic studies consider different levels of articulation of ideological thought: from fundamental assumptions about human nature and society to arguments about normative values to principles of action, policy positions and contextual responses to events (Scarbrough 1984, 26–39). Ideologies can also be analysed in terms of their conceptual structure. A particularly influential type of semantic analysis has been developed by Michael Freeden (1996). Freeden examines ideologies in terms of their 'morphology', namely as specific, distinctive configurations of mutually defining concepts. In Freeden's model each ideology consists of a cluster of 'core' concepts, linked with a set of (logically or culturally) 'adjacent' concepts, and a range of 'peripheral' concepts that are 'more specific and detailed' and usually situated 'on the perimeter of an ideology, between thought and action' (Freeden 2003, 62). Each ideology decontests, that is to say, assigns specific meanings to 'essentially contestable' political concepts (e.g., equality or liberty) and locates them in relationships with each other. Such conceptual arrangements are subject to variation, both synchronic (depending on local context) and diachronic (over time).

Turning to the historical analysis of ideology, it investigates how a given set of views came about, and it traces its evolution over time (Ball 1997). The focus is on continuity and change in political arguments and debates within and between different ideologies. The conceptual history approach is highly relevant to the argument advanced in this book. A point that I will often have occasion to stress here is that progressive opponents of neoliberalism tend to entertain a false sense of novelty and uniqueness as far as their ideas and strategies are concerned. Unwilling – as I will show anti-neoliberal activists and sympathetic intellectuals tend to be – to appreciate the extent of continuity between their own struggles against neoliberalism and those of previous generations of progressives against earlier forms of capitalism, they sometimes end up trying to 'reinvent the wheel'. One of the main contentions of this book is that, in view of its objectives, and also the obstacles that it faces, the present-day politics of resistance could learn and benefit from the broad and deep reservoir of progressive political thought.

Finally, the third type of analysis considers ideology's functions in shaping collective perceptions and actions. In epistemological terms, ideologies operate as affectively coloured cognitive frameworks that organize people's normative evaluations of political institutions and practices. Such evaluations are held, consciously or not, by individuals and groups in light of what they believe to be the most desirable models. A definition by anthropologist Clifford Geertz exemplifies this way of thinking. For Geertz, ideologies are 'maps of problematic social reality and matrices for the creation of collective conscience' – they 'render otherwise incomprehensible social situations meaningful, to so construe them as to make it possible to act purposefully within them' (Geertz 1964). Thus, moving on from consciousness to action, ideologies provide foundations for the formation and differentiation of political groups, including social movements, and fuel the competition between them. This function is played out on all levels of political contestation, from internal divisions within groups to more fundamental cleavages, such as neoliberalism versus the global justice movement (Zürn and de Wilde 2016). As David Apter put it in his 1964 work *Ideology and Discontent*, ideology 'dignifies discontent, identifies a target for grievances, and forms an umbrella over the discrete grievances of overlapping groups' (in Tarrow 2011, 31). Furthermore, it is in the light of specific political beliefs that legitimacy and authority are sustained or challenged, and thus, in this sense, ideologies may either support forces that conserve the existing system or, on the contrary, facilitate the disruption of power; the latter aspect of ideology is obviously of particular import for oppositional politics. While it is to be taken for granted that any social movement is ideological in nature, regardless of whether this inevitable quality is acknowledged by the group in question or not, I will argue that refusal to explicitly embrace ideology as a mobilizing and integrating tool has been a major liability for many anti-neoliberal movements.

The three approaches to ideology – semantic, historical and functional – do not, of course, operate in isolation from one another. Functional studies may occasionally proceed on a high level of generality in order to clarify the role of ideology per se in individual and collective affairs. However, such a broad analysis would normally need some supporting examples and so is usually accompanied by a semantic, meso- or micro-level, examination of specific ideological positions that help explain the reasons why a particular ideology-laden argument plays an important role for a given people at a given time. Thus, for instance, the appeal of an ideological interpretation may be explained by the match between, on the one hand, the followers' need for a convincing justification of their grievances or a broader meaningful contextualization explaining their current misfortunes and, on the other hand, the capacity of the given set of ideologically charged interpretations to provide just that. In the process of scholarly elucidation, references are made to relevant conceptual arrangements characteristic of the ideological system in question alongside considerations of the functions that ideology, understood in a generic way, fulfils. Furthermore, the diachronic dimension of analysis is normally taken into account as well, alongside semantic and functional examination, as it explains how the ideological interpretation in question has evolved historically and so helps to clarify what functions its previous forms fulfilled, or were expected to fulfil, and with what effect. Thus, the three aspects of analysis are likely to be involved, albeit in various proportions, in any given study. What connects the three approaches, as they are conceived here, is their shared assumption, which stems from and encapsulates the neutral perspective on ideology, that all perceptions of the political world are mediated by ideology and that, therefore, politics and ideology are inseparable.

While the neutral and inclusive way of thinking about ideology dominates in the mainstream study of political thought, it continues to be opposed by a range of critical approaches. As I have noted, the negative connotation of ideology has a long history. It goes back to Napoleon's politically motivated dismissal of Destutt de Tracy's 'science of ideas'. The pejorative interpretation of ideology received a particularly influential reinforcement in the work of Karl Marx and Friedrich Engels who incorporated the concept within their overall materialist rejection of philosophical idealism with its insistence on the import of ideas in historical development. What is more, Marx and Engels put forward a further set of arguments that critiqued ideology as a tool of distortion and exploitation operating on behalf of the dominant class in society, although not necessarily as an outcome of its consciously orchestrated efforts. In arguing the case for ideology as distorting social conditions, Marx and Engels famously used a comparison of ideology to *camera obscura*, a device that makes the world appear upside down (Marx and Engels 1970, 47). Accordingly, the ideological inversion of social reality serves as a major instrument of oppression. It perpetuates the rule of the dominant class by explaining the world in line with its interests: 'The ideas of the ruling class are in every epoch the ruling ideas, i.e., the class which is the ruling material force of society is at the same time its ruling intellectual force' (Marx and Engels 1970, 64). Consistently with the classical Marxist understanding of the term, 'working-class' or 'Marxist' ideology is an oxymoron. In keeping with Marx's vision of history, there will be no place for ideology in a communist society; the final stage of economic development will eliminate inequalities and contradictions of previous social formations, and so there will be no social injustice that would have to be obscured, legitimated or explained away by ideology.[1]

Interesting theories of ideology drawing on Marx's and Engels's key assumption of its distorting and oppressive function continue to be developed within Marxist and post-Marxist traditions of scholarship (Thompson 1990). However, the understanding of ideology that is typically held in anti-neoliberal activist circles does not follow the systematic Marxist critique. In fact, many activist and sympathetic accounts dismiss Marxism as itself an instance of 'ideological' thinking and describe the latter as doctrinaire, dogmatic and not in tune with the dynamism and diversity of the current repertoires of political action. Such interpretations have more in common with the arguments advanced against ideology by intellectuals associated with the political centre ground of the 1960s and, later, by neoliberals. As I will demonstrate shortly, the end of ideology claim was not part of the neoliberal lexicon until the early 1990s – before then neoliberals had shown a full appreciation of the role of ideology. In fact, the ground for neoliberalism's rise to hegemony in the 1970s had been in preparation through explicitly ideological means since at least the founding of the Mont Pèlerin society. When launching attacks from the political margins against what was the dominant way of thinking of the time, the protagonists of the neoliberal avant-garde were keen to put political ideas to action and openly committed themselves to a construction of a new ideology to challenge the status quo. But once neoliberalism attained the position of unquestioned hegemony from the 1970s onwards, its stance shifted markedly: Now the 'non-ideological' lingo of just doing 'what works' was mobilized to rationalize the profound transformation of society along neoliberal lines.

While neoliberalism has become the ruling ideology with non-ideological pretensions, its contestants have remained unwilling, or unable, to explicitly engage ideology in their attempts to challenge the neoliberal domination. Instead, the rebels ended up parroting much of the establishment's end of ideology discourse. Critiques of ideology, both mainstream and those invoked by progressive opponents of the powers that be, posit pragmatism and 'common sense' as the working principles for the post-ideological era that they assume to have arrived. The following section begins by considering the end of ideology claims of the 1960s and the successful destabilization of that consensus by neoliberalism. It then discusses the formation of neoliberalism's own end of ideology rhetoric and the way the latter has contributed to the ongoing weakness of anti-neoliberal politics which has unwittingly internalized much of its adversary's argumentation.

IDEOLOGY'S FOES AND FRIENDS: FROM THE POLITICS OF CONSENSUS TO THE END OF HISTORY

Ideology has become irretrievably fallen word. (Daniel Bell 1962, 447)

What to the contemporary observer appears as the battle of conflicting interests has indeed often been decided long before in a clash of ideas confined to narrow circles. (Hayek 1949, 372)

The early post–World War II decades were a time when the Keynesian combination of the market (where possible) and state intervention (where necessary) seemed to be the ultimate path to a prosperous future. Relying on that recipe, wealthy capitalist democracies thrived with high employment and a general sense of social security guaranteed by the welfare state. While the external threat in the form of the Soviet bloc persisted, internally the system seemed unchallengeable. The tragic legacy of Nazism and Stalinism led to the marginalization of political 'extremes' on the peripheries of the democratic society. The label of 'totalitarianism' (Friedrich and Brzezinski 1965) was applied to positions located at the two ends of the political spectrum, which was sometimes visualized as a horseshoe with the extremes close to each other, unlike on the conventional linear continuum. At the same time, it was a deeply conformist era with many of the identity-related concerns and campaigns that are commonplace today still in a germinal phase. Second-wave feminism, the gay movement, student protests, hippyism and movements promoting alternative lifestyles matured only in the mid-1960s; even the civil rights movement, although incipient already in the mid-1950s, did not come to a full swing until the 1963 March on Washington. The political debate of the 1950s was largely limited to how to manage the economy (rather than whether the latter should be subject to any bureaucratic management at all) and how to ensure that the state provides a maximum of social welfare for citizens (rather than whether the state should be in the business of providing such security in the first place). Moderate conservatives, modern liberals and social democrats were all in broad agreement on those general goals, even though their respective motives for becoming part of the 'politics of consensus' (Lane 1965) may have been different. Free-market ideas were not treated seriously as demonstrated by Hayek's academic marginalization at that time. Indeed, 'it was the free-marketers that were regarded as utopian outsiders, if not cranks' (Peck and Tickell 2007, 46).

It was in that prosperous, stable and conformist time that the end of ideology was announced by a number of prominent public intellectuals. Conservatives and modern liberals were particularly keen to declare their own positions to be non-ideological, common sense and pragmatic, merely accommodating to objective social circumstances and human nature. The trend was initiated by the American sociologist, Edward Shils. In his 1955 article 'End of Ideology?', Shils contrasted ideology with specific policy considerations pursued 'in a matter-of-fact way' (54). For Shils, non-ideological reasoning 'recognised no general principles and treated each emerging situation on its own merits' (54). 'We no longer feel the need for a comprehensive explicit system of beliefs', Shils asserted (57) at the same time reprimanding intellectuals for their 'rigidity, unwillingness to compromise, and . . . fear of being impure' (54). Similar points were made by the French scholar and columnist Raymond Aron (2011 [1957]) and by the American political sociologist Seymour Martin Lipset. Lipset posited that 'fundamental political problems of the industrial revolution have been solved', and hence the functional need for ideology had vanished and with it also 'domestic politics for those intellectuals who must have ideologies or Utopias to motivate them to political action' (1960, 406). He conceded that 'the democratic class struggle will continue' but insisted 'it will be a fight without ideologies' (1960, 408). What is often seen as the most important contribution to the debate, namely Daniel Bell's book *The End of Ideology*, was read along the same lines. Bell was later at pains to clarify that what he had meant to describe was the decline of Marxism (Bell 2000). But his book, as he complained afterwards (Bell 1988, 126), 'became better known for [its title] than [its] contents', and influenced the *zeitgeist* of that period accordingly. Meanwhile, Bell's association of the term *ideology* with political belief systems, primarily on the left, that demand a total transformation of society was taken up by others, notably the Australian conservative thinker Kenneth Minogue (1994).

Attitudes to ideology prevailing at that time among neoliberal outsiders were very different. While, as I will show, neoliberal luminaries and policy makers today disavow ideology, their forerunners contesting the Golden Age of Keynesian capitalism had a full appreciation for the power of ideas. The founders and early promoters of neoliberalism attached enormous significance to ideological struggle. Hayek, for example, argued that 'the free acceptance or rejection of ideas of the governing groups of the time' was the engine of history (Turner 2008, 69). When arguing in favour of taking political ideas seriously, Hayek often invoked the example of socialists, especially of the Fabian ilk. He admired socialists for their understanding of the importance of a good political argument and for their ideological persistence in the *Belle Époque* era of unbridled capitalism in late nineteenth and early twentieth centuries. In his essay titled 'The Intellectuals and Socialism' (1949), Hayek emphasized the ability of intellectuals, 'the second hand dealers in ideas' as he fondly dubbed them (371), to destabilize the consensus predominant at any given point in time through a long-term effort of constructing ideological counter-hegemony. It was instructive, Hayek thought, that socialism was primarily 'a construction of theorists, deriving from certain tendencies of abstract thought with which for a long time only the intellectuals were familiar; and it required long efforts by the intellectuals before the working classes could be persuaded to adopt it as their program' (371).

Hayek's acolytes took his insistence on ideological struggle seriously and drew practical organizational conclusions from it. Free-market think tanks started mushrooming challenging Keynesian capitalism almost as soon as it had consolidated itself as the dominant model. In 1955 the Institute of Economic Affairs (IEA) was established in London from where it still operates; it declares its mission to be 'to improve understanding of the fundamental institutions of a free society by analysing and expounding the role of markets in solving economic and social problems'. The formation of the IEA was later followed by others such as the Centre for Policy Studies opened by Margaret Thatcher and Keith Joseph in London in 1974 to accomplish, in Thatcher's words, 'the revival of the philosophy and principles of a free society, and the acceptance of it'. Another influential think tank, Adam Smith Institute, was created in 1977, also in London, and has since then been busy 'using free markets to create a richer, freer, happier world'. In the same year, Manhattan Institute came into being – it sees it as its mission 'to develop and disseminate new ideas that foster greater economic choice and individual responsibility'. Finally, to add one more example, National Center for Policy Analysis was founded in 1983 in Dallas with a goal 'to develop and promote private, free-market alternatives to government regulation and control, solving problems by relying on the strength of the competitive, entrepreneurial private sector'.[2] As Peck and Tickell (2007, 43) note, these think tanks 'were ideological in the sense that they were committed to a utopian vision of a free society, with liberated markets both reflecting and realizing individual choice and entrepreneurial effort, backed up by a minimalist government and the rule of law'.

Think tanks have been in the very centre of the process of production and dissemination of neoliberal ideology, and there is now an extensive literature documenting their beginnings in the 1950s and their rapid proliferation after neoliberalism's 'take off' in the mid-1970s (see, e.g., Cockett 1995; Mirowski and Plehwe 2009; Peck 2010; Stedman Jones 2012; Turner 2008). The importance of think tanks was appreciated so highly within neoliberal circles that resources were not spared to create, in 1981, the Atlas Economic Research Foundation whose specific purpose has been the formation and promotion of free-market think tanks all over the world. Furthermore, the ideological production and dissemination of neoliberalism extended to the world of mass media, where newspapers like *The Times*, *The Economist* and *The Daily Telegraph* proved particularly favourable platforms (Peck and Tickell 2007, 40). Naturally, the fervent activity of neoliberal intellectuals continued also in the world of academia, with the

Chicago School of Economics as the leading neoliberal intellectual centre in the United States forging talents intended both for the domestic needs and for export (Nik-Khan and Van Horn 2016).

The neoliberal journey to hegemony took approximately three decades and required patience and unwavering commitment to what seemed like a distant utopia. Hayek accepted that freeing the market from the state would be 'a long-run effort, concerned not so much with what would be immediately practicable, but with the beliefs which must gain ascendence' (in Srnicek and Williams 2015, 55). Milton Friedman, another leading free-market intellectual and also a Noble laureate (two years after Hayek), made a similar point: 'Our basic function [is] to develop alternatives to existing policies, to keep them alive and available until the politically impossible becomes the politically inevitable' (Friedman 2002 [1962], xiv). And, indeed, when the time came, marked by stagflation, the early 1970s oil shocks, increased labour militancy and the overall sense of crisis afflicting the Keynesian model, then the free marketeers were there, ready to seize the opportunity – something that the left has proved unprepared to do in the wake of the recent dramatic convulsions of neoliberalism.

Once the idea that markets are always right established itself as the economic orthodoxy in the way that I described in chapter 1, neoliberal intellectuals started drifting away from an overt commitment to ideological work. A new wave of 'endism' (Huntington 1989) began to rise and reached peak proportions in the early 1990s amid the disintegration of Soviet communism. It owed its main articulation to the neoconservative thinker Francis Fukuyama whose take on ideology was somewhat different from the typical obituaries for it written in the 1950s and 1960s. Fukuyama's theory was about 'the end of history' by which he meant, in a quasi-Hegelian manner, 'the endpoint of mankind's ideological evolution' (1989, 4). According to Fukuyama, 'What is emerging victorious . . . is not so much liberal practice, as the liberal *idea*. That is to say, for a very large part of the world, there is now no ideology with pretensions to universality that is in a position to challenge liberal democracy' (Fukuyama 1992, 45, emphasis in original). In other words, while not denying its ideological nature, Fukuyama announced 'an unabashed victory of economic and political liberalism' (1989, 1) and hence the end of ideological debate. But regardless of the content or logic of Fukuyama's argument, it has invigorated the broader end of ideology sentiment which now combined confidence about liberalism unchallengeable position with old claims about ideology as a 'typically dogmatic, i.e., rigid and impermeable, approach to politics' (Sartori 1969, 402).

This rejuvenated end of ideology vernacular is no longer confined to abstruse academic debates – it has been popularized very effectively by mainstream politicians and opinion makers. From the 1990s onwards, the discourse of alleged necessity, pragmatism, just doing 'what works' has pervaded the political communication of both neoconservative right and the Third Way neoliberal 'left', especially the branch of it associated with the British sociologist Anthony Giddens and his friends: Tony Blair and Bill Clinton. More recent examples of this rhetoric include the declarations by Barack Obama (2009b): 'What is required is a new declaration of independence, not just in our nation, but in our own lives – from ideology and small thinking', and by former British Prime Minister David Cameron (2010): 'We are not driven by some theory or some ideology. . . . We are doing this [austerity] because we have to'. A highly dismissive and negative view of ideology features also in the 2017 Manifesto of the British Conservative Party (9): 'We see rigid dogma and ideology not just as needless but dangerous'. This is just a recent instance of the long-standing 'non-ideological' posture of the Conservatives. For example, in the 1979 Manifesto of the party Margaret Thatcher wrote: 'The heart of politics is not political theory, it is people and how they want to live their lives' (Thatcher 1979). But while many more examples could be listed here, the main point is to note their function. Such assertions aim to make global capitalism seem as inevitable as the weather and thus to dissimulate, naturalize and dehistoricize the world system of today.

Neoliberals have been impressively successful in making their ideas appear as natural and common sense even to their staunch opponents. There are, to be sure, some who see through the neoliberal 'no ideology' discursive tactic. For example, the leader of the Spanish leftist, anti-austerity party *Podemos* ('We Can'), Pablo Iglesias (2015, 17), is quite clear on the point that 'the most important ideological operations are those that give the appearance of being non-ideological to notions that are perceived as common sense'. However, this insight does not seem to be shared by many on the anti-neoliberal left. In fact, it is a striking manifestation of neoliberalism's hegemony that assumptions informing its end of ideology thesis have received ample articulation across the entire spectrum of the current debate within and about progressive activism. This may certainly seem ironic in view of the anti-systemic credentials of most of the literature in question. One explanation of the paradox lies in the fact that anti-neoliberal movements operate within the parameters of the current capitalist system which imposes limits on what is deemed politically viable. The constraints are of diverse nature: structural, but ideational too in that neoliberal capitalism also shapes the concepts and discourses with which people endeavour to comprehend the political world. In other words, the counter-hegemonic activism of today is subject to the super-structural impact of the dominant ideology, and so aspects of the neoliberal view of the world filter through the movement's conceptual dimension in often concealed and hence intractable ways. But, in any case, the end of ideology is a hoax, intellectually and politically, and the welcoming reception that this notion has received on the anti-neoliberal left continues to exert a paralysing influence on the latter. The next section provides a preliminary sketch of the nature and implications of the end of ideology claim as it is articulated in the literature concerned with and usually coming from within the anti-neoliberal movement.[3]

END OF IDEOLOGY AND ITS UNLIKELY ENTHUSIASTS

We are not interested in ideology anymore – we just want things to work properly and fairly. (Cocker 2012)

Celebratory assertions of ideology's irrelevance were put forward in the course of the 1990s and early 2000s by activists, intellectuals and popularizers of global justice or alter-globalist movements and continued into the recent phase of anti-neoliberal mobilization culminating in the Occupy movement. This particular end of ideology verdict is not meant to suggest an exhaustion of radical politics. However, it bears a resemblance to mainstream neoliberal obituaries for ideology in that it proclaims it to be redundant in political practice: 'Many groupings within the anti-capitalist movement are evidently either *non-ideological* or *post-ideological*. This is to say that there are groupings that are quite explicitly opposed to the idea that what the movement needs is an alternative vision of how the world should look' (Tormey 2004, 75).

An example of a particularly unequivocal refutation of ideology is Giorel Curran's book about what she calls 'anti-globalization'. Much of Curran's discussion is devoted to the idea that anarchism, a key influence in movements under her investigation, has become post-ideological. In suggesting that anarchism has been able to free itself from 'ideological conformity' (2006, 6), Curran's argument illustrates the reasoning that is common in the literature preoccupied with popular challenges to neoliberalism. Unflattering semantic associations attached to the concept of ideology are commonplace in such interpretations. Ideology is identified with rigidity; adjectives such as 'doctrinaire', 'sectarian', 'conformist', 'vanguardist' and 'orthodox' are used to describe politics that is 'ideological'. On the other hand, 'general spirit' and 'inspiration' are said to characterize the 'vibrant' 'post-ideological' positions that are credited with the ability to come together and challenge neoliberal capitalism (Curran 2006, 1–16). In other sources, 'rigid' ideologies are also contrasted with a more 'practical' focus on political effectiveness. For example, Donatella della Porta reports that participants of Social Forums in Europe 'avoid ideologism' and 'instead present their action as *pragmatic, concrete, and gradualist*' (della Porta 2005, 196, emphasis in original). Massimo De Angelis likewise insists that what matters for 'today's new internationalism is not a common ideology, but needs and the practical necessities of different movements within the context of the global economy' (De Angelis 2000, 9). But De Angelis also uses more evocative terms when contrasting a 'predefined Ideology' with '*what is here and now to be lived: dignity, hope, life*' (2000, 26, capitalization and emphasis in original).

Post-ideology claims have often been made with regard to specific political positions engaged in the contestation of neoliberal globalization (Curran's book provides one example). In other words, ideology is acknowledged as a feature in some segments of the politics of anti-neoliberalism, but not in others. Thus, for instance, Geoffrey Pleyers suggests a distinction between two broad options within 'alter-globalization'. The 'way of subjectivity' adheres to the values of creativity and autonomy and the need to eschew the established protocols of mainstream politics. On the other hand, the 'way of reason' accentuates 'the logic of expertise', rationality and organization (Pleyers 2010, 142, 137). The 'way of subjectivity' is described by Pleyers as 'more pragmatic and less ideological', occurring 'outside grand ideologies', while the 'way of reason' is 'more political' and 'vanguard' in nature (2010, 137, 87, 142, 226). Overall, according to Pleyers, 'Alterglobalization has entered a new phase, more focused on obtaining concrete results than on struggling over ideas' (2010, 249). The contrast, evident also in previous examples, between ideology and 'getting things done' is untenable from the perspective of the neutral approach which assumes that all political action is irrevocably tied with ideology in that ideological frameworks inform the pursuit of specific political results, while the results in turn get interpreted in light of political ideas. Pleyers's account is characteristic of the attitude to ideology that prevails in the literature on anti-neoliberalism. As a further example, the discussion of 'global justice networks' by Paul Routledge and Andrew Cumbers (2009, 48) also falls into the fallacy of distinguishing established ideological currents from what they call 'post-ideological (e.g., autonomist) positionalities'. Simon Tormey's typology of 'anti-capitalist' positions likewise includes 'ideological/affirmative' and 'post/non-ideological negative' categories (Tormey 2004).

These examples draw on the 'alter-globalization' phase on anti-neoliberal activism, but connotations and style of end of ideology claims remain similar in arguments revolving around more recent movements. For example, a manifesto published on Facebook in 2010 by a leading activist of the *Democracia Real YA* network (from which the *Indignados* evolved) proclaimed: 'This is not a movement of the Left or of the Right. We do not adhere to any theoretical groupuscule, be it Marxist, neo-Leninist, or anarchist. We are *simply* young people' (in Gerbaudo 2012, 83, emphasis in original). Pablo Gerbaudo (2012, 83) notes that this refusal to identify with ideology and political categories such as left and right became a major characteristic of *Democracia Real YA* and its offshoots. The Occupy has been described in similar terms. For example, in the words of Neil Howard and Keira Pratt-Boyden, it represented 'fluid, undefined social movements . . . which aim to be free of ideological or institutional constraint'; its 'activists affiliate through solidarity, which transcends ideologies' and have, overall, 'more nuanced attitudes towards politics' (Howard and Pratt-Boyden 2013, 733, 734). Typical of some of these arguments is their vagueness as when Occupy's pluralism is said to replace ideological identities 'with identifications with the social whole' (Jones 2014, 156). Others have exceeded in enthusiasm with which they have pronounced ideology's death. An exultant prose by Michael Hardt and Antonio Negri epitomizes this; referring to Occupy, the two veteran intellectuals of anti-neoliberal movements exclaim (2012, 107): 'The streets are full but the churches are empty. . . . The churches are empty in the sense that, although there is a lot of fight in these movements, there is little ideology or centralized political leadership'. They then go on: 'We need to empty the churches of the Left even more, and bar their doors, and burn them down! . . . The movement's slogans and arguments have spread so widely not despite but because the positions they express cannot be summarized or disciplined in a fixed ideological line'.

This 'no ideology' position is obviously flawed. To reiterate, ideology is inextricably linked with power and its legitimization, and with protest, resistance and other dimensions of political activism (for British examples, see Ibrahim 2013). This comprises any aspect of social movements' formation and life cycle – their discourses, strategies, successes and failures. Ideology is certainly not dead. However, as Pamela Oliver and Hank Johnston (2005, 195) put it, 'what seems out of fashion right now is overt public discussion in terms of ideology, that is, in terms of theories of society coupled with explicit discussion of values and norms'. Thus, the issue at hand boils down to the fact that the movements in question are not particularly preoccupied with *explicit* ideological work: 'Left-wing and progressive radical politics today do not, in general, offer *grand visions* for change. . . . There is no obvious alternative overarching plan for society, coming from the Left and progressives' (Pugh 2009, 4, emphasis in original). The majority of movement insiders, including many academics, believe that this lack of interest in ideology is a good thing as it liberates the movements from the ideational straitjacket that ideology allegedly imposes. Critics, like myself, who are far fewer and farther between, emphasize the weaknesses that this approach produces, namely lack of focus, ephemerality of struggles, neutralization and unwitting susceptibility to recuperation and co-optation, or mere 'selective facilitation' (Tarrow 2011, 209), by neoliberalism:

> After the supposed purity of properly ideological politics comes, not a post-ideological, postmodern politics, but a politics in which deep ideological commitment is disavowed and cast into the unconscious, where, of course, it is a far

more powerful and less reflexive drive to everyday conformist action. Ideology is still, quite clearly, operative on the field of politics. Now, however, it works its magic behind the scenes. (Winlow et al. 2015, 166)

In chapters that follow I will have many occasions to elaborate on these and other repercussions of the tendency to relegate ideology to the unacknowledged background of political action. What is required at this point is a preliminary contextualization of some socio-political trends and intellectual fashions that have contributed to the left's post-ideological posture. Of course, as already noted, the influence of neoliberalism is the most important reason for the pervasive turn away from (overt) ideology: Neoliberal claims concerning ideology have been absorbed by its challengers uncritically and inadvertently, in a manner that illustrates how hegemony operates. But while the depoliticizing impact of neoliberalism is of central significance and so is discussed at several key junctures of the argument advanced in this book, there are also factors indigenous to the territory of the left, notably postmodernism and identitarian politics, that have made substantial inputs into the left's post-ideological outlook. They therefore require at least a brief consideration.

Postmodernism avows 'the decline of the unifying and legitimating power of the grand narratives' (Lyotard 1984 [1979], 38), and there is a strong postmodern inclination evident in both social movement theory and activism to celebrate the particular, the local and the unique and reject any notion of a defined structure or political unity. As Jeremy Gilbert (2008, 101–2) notes, postmodern writers – Gilles Deleuze, Michel Foucault and Jean-François Lyotard among others – 'move away from any notion of society as a totality. They reject any view which would conceptualise social relations within a given context as constituting a singular whole governed by an overarching force, principle or historical destiny' (Gilbert 2008, 101–2). A pertinent expression of the attitude described by Gilbert is Richard Rorty's distinction between 'movements' and 'campaigns' (1995). Accordingly, what Rorty calls 'movements' are overarching social mobilizations that orient political action towards totalizing and teleological visions of humankind's development. 'Campaigns', on the other hand, revolve around specific and delimited issues and do not posit a comprehensive model of a different society (congruent with the postmodern orientation, Rorty's support was with the politics of campaigns). This is a popular but problematic dichotomy. Any political argument, not just those involved in what postmodernists dismiss as grand, all-encompassing deliberations, is ideology-laden; political positions on particular issues are not stand-alone, matter-of-fact statements but are imbued with meaning in the context of ideological values held, knowingly or not, by their proponents. In other words, any specific 'campaign' has to be justified not just on its own terms but also on a wide-ranging ideational background that frames its grievances and demands. Political debates and struggles, both those of a broad nature and those focused on 'single issues', are inevitably mediated by ideology; 'the facts do not speak for themselves: we speak for them' (Goodwin 2016, 32), and we do so on the basis of our ideology-laden beliefs whether acknowledged or followed on a more emotive, subconscious level.

Postmodernism has left a lasting impact on the way in which anti-neoliberal movements perceive themselves and are described by the major-ity of their scholarly spokespersons. There is a general tendency in relevant literature to endorse the abandonment by the movements of any attempts to come together in a counter-hegemonic effort based on shared objectives and visions. The trend is exemplified by an enthusiastic assertion coming from an anthropologist and grass-roots activist, Marianne Maeckelbergh: 'There is no singular goal, adversary, or identity that is shared by all movement actors except at the most abstract level of desiring "(an)other world(s)"' (2011, 1–2). Instead of a pursuit of an ideological common ground, however general, the emphasis of post-ideology claims tends to be on unities so diluted that they do not form any proper basis for a counter-hegemonic formation. These include insignificant methodological commonalities touted as stemming from the networked nature of contemporary activism ('insignificant', as chapter 3 will substantiate, because networking is not a meaningful distinction; it applies to all kinds of organizational logic nowadays), or ludic and spontane-ous nature of the movements' prefigurative actions (a weakness, as chapter 4 will argue, unless activism is not expected to have any broader social impact), or populist narratives, such as the 99 percent (which, as chapter 5 will docu-ment, have been left undeveloped beyond a basic expression of anger with how things are).

The postmodern rejection of universalism and the related scepticism about any mass-scale, goal-orientated social action is related to the rise, primar-ily from the 1960s onwards, of identitarian politics that revolves around the interests of particular groups defined by ethnicity, religion, gender, sexual orientation or other criteria of distinction and marginalization. The problem here is that political mobilization that proceeds primarily on the basis of affirmation of difference, and with emphasis on multiple claims of separate and often rival groups, may lead to fracturing of the collective power and turn groups inwards rather than forging any productive alliances between them. With regard to large-scale, popular social mobilizations, like the incredibly diverse and syncretized anti-neoliberal 'movement', the focus on the politics of identity may result in their inability to formulate any demands. In the eyes of its critics, identitarian fragmentation prevents articulation of shared goals or strategies and 'becomes moralistic, stultifyingly bound up with expressions of political correctness, such that robust independent thinking on the Left virtually disappears for fear of offending someone's precious sense of self-identity' (McLennan 2009, 46). The radical pluralism of contemporary social movements – where 'each societal practice, each discourse, if it is to be understood at all, is to be understood in its own terms' (Scott 1990, 102) – leaves them unable to advance any effective counter-hegemonic agenda.

In addition to a nonchalant repudiation by many movement articulators of any need for an organizing ideology,[4] the shift towards identity politics has also entailed a neglect of the key issues of political economy and so left that field pretty much open for neoliberal takeover. 'Post-materialism' (Inglehart 1971) has long been a leading theme in social movement studies and, congruently, the significance of class-based or economically motivated mobilizations has been downplayed in favour of the activism that relies on the 'power of identity' (Castells 2010b). Recent critiques of this tendency lament the 'disappearance of capitalism' (e.g., della Porta 2015; Hetland and Goodwin 2013; Rosenhek and Shalev 2013; Silver and Karatasli 2015). Where the focus on identity issues contributes to the neglect of the politics of antagonism that revolves around the opposition between capital and labour, an unintended result may be an obfuscation of the class nature of neoliberalism's power. And, further, neoliberalism may also benefit discursively when emancipatory struggles of identitarian movements end up 'supplying a portion of the "new spirit" or charismatic rationale for a new mode of capital accumulation, touted as "flexible", "difference-friendly", "encouraging of creativity from below"' (Fraser 2013, 130).

Ultimately, the issue at stake is that their postmodern predisposition and identitarian fragmentation, in combination with the abandonment of overt ideology, mean that anti-neoliberal movements are less able to confront the powerful, complex and global system of neoliberal capitalism. After all, it is clear that they cannot match the material might of neoliberalism's main constituencies, the corporation and the transnational capitalist class, and so the main asset that they are left with is their capacity to think beyond what is empirically given and their power to shape people's imagination. The left used to excel in terms of its ability to carve out compelling ideological visions. Unfortunately, for some time now, left-wing progressivism has been punching below its ideational weight. The sweeping repudiation of 'ideological politics', parroted by anti-neoliberals after the very hegemonic discourse that they want to target, has led many anti-neoliberal movements to seek ersatz refuge in the celebration of networking, prefigurative politics and vague populism. Chapter 3, concerned with the practices and discourses of networking, embarks on a detailed discussion of what is, in some respects, one of the dead ends of progressive politics today.

NOTES

1. Marx's and Engels's insights into the nature of ideology provided inspiration for a long succession of activists and scholars some of whom – notably Vladimir Lenin, Antonio Gramsci and Karl Mannheim – modified the original Marxian model of ideology away from its emphasis on the inextricable link with capitalism and towards a more inclusive conception, whereby ideology is viewed as reflective of the material reality of *any* social environment. Such thinkers also argued, often by qualifying the concept in various ways, that the subordinate classes could, and should, develop their own counter-ideologies.

2. Quoted from the think tanks' mission statements available online (all accessed 27 June 2017): https://iea.org.uk/about-us; http://www.cps.org.uk/about/; https://www.adamsmith.org/; https://www.manhattan-institute.org/; http://www.ncpa.org/about/.

3. Much of the literature discussed in this book has hybrid nature in that it brings together activist and academic insights. The academic literature on anti-neoliberal movements is less 'grass-roots', and less ephemeral, than the activist communication found on the web, particularly on social networking sites but retains insider status. Most contributors 'present the movements in their own words and by their own actions' (Castells 2015, 18). Others assume a degree of critical distance but still identify with the politics of resistance – in other words, they are critical 'as insiders' (Graeber 2009, 12, see also Bray 2013; Juris 2008; Juris and Khasnabish 2013). There is no need to draw sharp distinctions between the two, activist and academic, currents of reflection: Scholarly authors themselves are keen to declare that their perspective is not one 'of the theorist removed and separate from organizing but rather from within' (Shukaitis and Graeber 2007, 11) and thereby straddles the worlds of activism and academia. Such authors can thus be seen as 'organic intellectuals' who navigate the interface between political commitment and professional academic engagement. Of course, the academic value of research conducted from a position of advocacy is a separate question as is its utility to the movements that the 'activist scholars' claim to represent (for a discussion of this issue, see Gillan and Pickerill 2012).

4. A parallel shift in the field of social movement studies away from the concept of ideology and towards a more 'neutral', but also in some respects inadequate, notion of 'frames' demonstrates the pariah-like status of 'ideology' in some corners of social science (Oliver and Johnston 2005).

Chapter 3

Networking and Its Pitfalls

The celebration of the end of ideology that characterizes anti-neoliberal discourses goes hand in hand with an ardent belief in the supreme role fulfilled in political activism by the information and communication technology (ICT). This chapter examines the connections between the two sets of assumptions. It begins by considering a broader debate on shifting technological paradigm and its political and economic consequences. The focus is then narrowed to claims about the ICT that are articulated within or in relation to anti-neoliberal movements. My contention is that while the ICT has undoubtedly helped some aspects of activism, the dominant tendency to reify technology has obfuscated the dynamics of political action. By disengaging activists from debates about the values and goals of political activism, the overriding fixation with technology has reinforced the flawed perception that ideology has little relevance for anti-neoliberal movements.

CONTOURS OF THE DEBATE

A free-flowing network of communications may be exactly what takes us to the next stage of human development. Some have called the Internet the nervous system of the planet. It becomes harder to dehumanise when all of us are on the same network. Like the right hand declaring war on the left hand. This could be the system by which we take the next leap of evolution and move from a divided to a united species. (Brooke 2012, 238)

In 1996, when a group of high-profile digerati took to the pages of *Wired* magazine and proclaimed that the 'public square of the past' was being replaced by the Internet, a technology that 'enables average citizens to participate in national discourse, publish a newspaper, distribute an electronic pamphlet to the world . . . while simultaneously protecting their privacy', many historians must have giggled. From the railways, which Karl Marx believed would dissolve India's caste system, to television, the great-est liberator of the masses, there has hardly appeared a technology that wasn't praised for its ability to raise the level of public debate, introduce more transparency into politics, reduce nationalism, and transport us to the mythical global village. In virtually all cases, such high hopes were crushed by the brutal forces of politics, culture, and economics. Technolo-gies, it seems, tend to overpromise and underdeliver, at least on their initial promises. (Morozov 2011, 275)

The tendency to view anti-neoliberal movements as post-ideological is part of a broader trend to see ours as an age marked by changes so far-reaching that they cannot be explained, let alone tackled, by established repertoires of concepts or measures. In other words, the paradigm has changed and the ways of conceptualizing social realities that we have inherited from the allegedly bygone era of modernity no longer work. This sweeping conclusion brings many social movement scholars together with theorists of postmod-ernism as well as some leading voices in globalization studies. At the heart of arguments suggesting such a fundamental and comprehensive shift are exponential advances, over the past three decades, in the ICT (an overview of relevant debates is available in Dutton 2013). The many impacts of the ICT are typically discussed in connection with its ontological repercussions, namely what Manuel Castells (2010a, 2010b) calls the 'space of flows'. In the words of Felix Stadler (2001), this 'emerged when it became necessary and possible to integrate entities that are physically far apart into the single units than can work in real time'. The process of 'respatialization' (Scholte 2005), it has been professed, undermines the conventional Euclidean logic and with it the territorial 'space of places' (Castells 2010a) marking 'a new ontology of place/space relations' (Amin 2002, 385) or even 'the end of geography' (O'Brien 1992). Specialized literatures examine how multiple implications of this spatial shift affect governance, economy, culture and social inquiry itself.

There are certainly good reasons for the amount of attention that the ICT has received from all branches of social sciences. There is no denying that the ICT has played a role in major political events, beginning with the collapse of statist communism in the Soviet Union and its Central and Eastern European satellite regimes, as well as facilitating the meteoric rise of international non-governmental organizations. Furthermore, in economic terms, the possibility of cheap real-time communication across any distance has enabled outsourc-ing of many processes and segments of capitalist production. The increased mobility of capital and hence a more effective externalizing of its costs, along with an assumed weakening of state-managed regulatory mechanisms, have given capitalism a more unapologetic face and have been linked to rising inequality, within nations and globally, and unprecedented environmental degradation worldwide, not to mention again the recurrent crises that culminated with the 2007–2008 credit crunch. Finally, last but not least, it is important to also consider the role of the ICT in popular mobilizations against those evils – the protests have been supported, to an extent, by new communication tools that proved able, now and then, to circumvent control by the authorities.

However, notwithstanding its vital importance in what is described, in a clichéd manner, as the 'Information Age' (Castells 2010a, 2010b), technology is a risky concept as it is highly susceptible to reification (Marx 2001; Morozov 2011, 94). Its impact on society tends to be elevated above, and seen as overriding, other factors – ideas, other dimensions of culture, political and economic constraints and opportunities and so on – and such a disproportionate emphasis on technology may obscure the complex nature of social life. In the prevailing overly deterministic interpretations, technology is presented as embodying society itself, or as a mould in which society is cast, rather than a product of social forces, amenable to human influence but also tending to serve specific interests of particular groups. The old dictum that 'the medium is the message' is often assumed to apply in an unequivocal manner, and the ICT is consequently viewed as a – if not the – determinant of what is culturally, politically and socially possible.

There are two broad variants of this technological determinism, each coming in a number of different shades and intensities. On the one hand, in a pessimistic take on it, the ICT has a profoundly dehumanizing influence. The cyberpunk genre of literature and film represents an extreme version of such pessimism; it paints a vision of the world in which artificial intelligence encapsulated in cyberspace, or 'matrix', threatens to eliminate or paralyse human agency. Technology is thus reified and turned into a bearer of dystopian projections of the future with no due consideration of other social dynamics. On the other hand, optimistic interpretations celebrate the ICT as a powerful force for good without paying adequate attention to its nuanced and often ambiguous outcomes that depend on specific situation and purpose to which it is put, as well as ignoring the broader context, particularly the issue of access, control and overall political economy within which technology operates.

This, of course, is not a new controversy. Major technological transitions in the past caused similar polarizations of opinions and concomitant social struggles, as exemplified by the clash between the beneficiaries of the Industrial Revolution and the Luddites, an early nineteenth-century movement of English textile makers against the introduction of weaving machinery that reduced the need for human labour in the industry (Sale 1995). Contrasting arguments and visions pertaining to the Internet itself go back to the 1990s. In 1996, just five years after the World Wide Web became available to the public, John Perry Barlow (one of the founders of a digital rights group, the Electronic Frontier Foundation) published 'A Declaration of Independence of Cyberspace'. The document, which has been reproduced on thousands of websites, asserts that 'Governments of the Industrial World' have no sovereignty over the Internet: 'You have no moral right to rule us nor do you possess any methods of enforcement we have true reason to fear'. This vision of a democratic and egalitarian electronic world 'that all may enter without privilege or prejudice accorded by race, economic power, military force, or station of birth' (Barlow 1996), was then (in)famously challenged by two hackers, known as Acid Phreak and Phiber Optik, who did not recognize the representation of the collaborative electronic space and 'virtual community' (Rheignold 1998) advanced by Barlow and other techno-utopians. Instead, Acid Phreak and Phiber Optik projected a predatory image of cyberspace as a domain of corporate control and surveillance. The two made their points remarkably concrete by hacking into the database of a credit records holding company and publicly revealing the details of Barlow's credit history held by the firm (Turner 2010, 168).

More recent opinions concerning the nature and implications of the ICT remain sharply divided. Among the optimists are journalists, like Heather Brooke who speaks emphatically of 'a new Information Enlightenment' (2012, ix), as well as academics, including Manuel Castells and Clay Shirky, not to mention the voices of ICT industry captains. From this point of view, the ICT is a 'liberation technology' (Diamond 2016, 132–46) that marks a completely new era in the history of humankind and opens unprecedented political opportunities. The degree of enthusiasm goes from considerable to overwhelming. Shirky's position is broadly right, though not extremely enlightening, when he argues that 'as more people adopt simple social tools, and as those tools allow increasingly rapid communication, the speed of group actions also increases' (2008, 161). He certainly sounds temperate in comparison with Brooke's assertion (2012, ix): 'We are at an extraordinary moment in human history: never before has the possibility of true democracy been so close to realisation'. But while Brooke writes as a journalist, which may help explain the hype, Castells's excitement does not fall far behind. He avows that 'networked social movements' will bring about significant social changes 'because the current political institutions, almost everywhere, are ineffective and illegitimate in the minds of their citizens. Minds that are being opened up by the winds of free communication and inspire practices of empowerment enacted by fearless youth' (Castells 2015, 312). Furthermore, the change that is eagerly anticipated by ICT enthusiasts will not be limited to political protocols. As 'the traditional gatekeepers of power have now seen the full revolutionary force of the Internet' (Brooke 2012, 243), political transformation will be just the first step towards a profound egalitarian restructuring of society: 'Technology is breaking down traditional barriers of status, class, power, wealth and geography, replacing them with an ethos of collaboration and transparency' (Brooke 2012, ix).

Where optimists see the democratizing force of the Internet, pessimists discern a new apparatus of surveillance (Andrejevic 2005; Christensen 2011), or even a springboard for a more effective form of authoritarianism (Morozov 2011). While striving to debunk the 'myth' of democracy on the web (Hindman 2009), sceptics also downplay its long-term mobilizing potential with regard to political activism (Gerbaudo 2012). And whereas enthusiasts celebrate what they see as an unprecedented opening, afforded by the ICT, for a shift towards greater equality and justice, critics speak of 'cyberapartheid' (Putnam 2000, 175) and draw attention to how the Internet, and unequal access to it, 'reproduces – and facilitates – the dynamics of secession, exclusion and segmentation' (Gitlin 1998, 172).

So the jury is out, and will most likely remain out, on whether the ICT is humankind's saviour or a harbinger of an impending civilizational Armageddon. In any case, as per usual, the truth is likely to be somewhere in between the two extremes. However, a broader point is that technological determinism, whether optimistic or not, may lead to an outcome that has been elucidated by a researcher of new technologies, Evgeny Morozov (after Raymond Williams). Morozov writes:

> Placing technology at the center of our intellectual analysis is bound to make us view what we have traditionally understood as a problem of politics, with its complex and uneasy questions of ethics and morality, as instead a problem of technology, either eliminating or obfuscating all the unresolved philosophical dilemmas. (Morozov 2011, 292)

This observation is apt as to the debates within and about anti-neoliberal movements. These movements have both benefitted from and encouraged the development of the Internet throughout its history.[1] However, as I will argue, their disproportionate preoccupation with technological tools of political action has led them to a number of problematic outcomes, including ignorance of the need for an explicit political vision to motivate and guide the action.

Deliberations on the relationship between the ICT and activism have evolved over time. A noticeable trend within the debate is that whereas it used to be dominated by passionate all-out assertions of a comprehensive, technologically enabled, transformation of political activism, more cautious and balanced arguments have gained some ground of late (particularly once recent waves of anti-neoliberal mobilization – the Arab Spring, the *Indignados* and the Occupy movement – came and went without causing any fundamental disruption to how the global neoliberal system operates). But while the debate on the ICT and activism seems to have matured, it has not, on the whole, considered the question of ideology to be of much relevance. This gap should be addressed: Bringing ideology into the discussion sheds light on some of the implications of technological reductionism. In particular, a proper reflection on ideology lends support to broader critiques regarding two sets of convictions – of strategic uniqueness and horizontality – that the technological fixation has engendered within the ranks of anti-neoliberal activists. The next section explores these two fallacies of anti-neoliberal techno-centrism and highlights their relationship with problematic approaches to ideology.

UNIQUENESS, HORIZONTALITY AND OTHER FANTASIES

> Technology, like gas, will fill in any conceptual space provided. (Morozov 2011, 294)

The claim to uniqueness due to an ingenious use of technology has been part and parcel of anti-neoliberal activist discourse from its early 'alter-globalization' phase onwards. 'Networks' and 'networking', in particular, have been turned into key buzzwords in debates within and about anti-neoliberal activism,[2] not just with regard to the movements' tactics and strategies but also as an allegedly fundamental characteristic of their overall political identity. Broadly speaking, the argument is that since networking involves a new mode of communication between activists, it therefore engenders an unprecedented type of movement:

> The characteristics of communication processes between individuals engaged in the social movement determine the organizational characteristics of the social movement itself. . . . This is why the networked social movements of the digital age represent a new species of social movement. (Castells 2015, 15)

According to such accounts, networking brings about a powerful form of activism, one that is not subject to constraints that used to limit political resistance in the past. Epitomizing this way of thinking, Hardt and Negri (2000, 25) posit (after Gilles Deleuze and Félix Guatarri) that 'resistances are no longer marginal but active in the center of a society that opens up in networks; the individual points are singularized in a thousand plateaus'. A popular writer and broadcaster, Paul Mason (2016, xvii) follows a similar vein when he asserts that networks 'cannot be silenced or dispersed'. Examples that such accounts use as their support span more than two decades, extending from the 1994 Zapatista uprising which, according to one commentator, established a 'participatory, synergistic and cybernetic feedback' between itself and the world 'leading to an explosion of creativity and of civil society' (Martinez-Torres 2001), to Arab Spring, 'planned on Facebook, organised on Twitter and broadcast to the world via You Tube' (Mason 2012, 14), to Occupy which 'was born on the Internet, diffused by the Internet and maintained its presence on the Internet' (Castells 2015, 171). But the zenith of this ICT mania came with the eruption of the Arab Spring (preceded by the 2009 protests in Iran). The names of the main social networking platforms, Facebook and Twitter, became routinely attached to the wave of uprisings against both autocracy and neoliberalism in the Arab World even though access to the Internet in countries like Iran or Egypt was inadequate to render Facebook or Twitter the main tools of mobilization there (Morozov 2009b, 12).[3] Initially a part of the mainstream media's catalogue of favourite catchphrases (Cohen 2011; Webster 2011), discourses of 'Facebook Revolutions' or 'Twitter Protests' soon became popular in academic and activist accounts of anti-neoliberal resistance (Lim 2012).[4]

While attractive to what is a predominantly youthful movement, the notion that networking confers on anti-neoliberal movements some ontological or ethical distinctiveness, or provides them with extraordinary strategic advantages, is misleading. The degree of saturation of the world today by the electronic media means that it is naïve of activists to view themselves as exceptional in that respect. As Fenton and Barassi (2011, 190) argue, 'In a world of communicative abundance, putting one's political faith in the ability of individual instances of communicative experience, albeit in a networked form, to deliver social and political change, is a dubious practice' (see also Boggs 2012, 164; Dean 2009, 49; Morozov 2009a, 2009b). However, the substance of the predicament is not just information or communication overload. The issue goes further in that, in contrast with many activist and academic opinions, networks 'are not a natural enemy of the status quo' (Gladwell 2010). Actually, the sphere of electronic communication is deeply penetrated by the logic of neoliberal capitalism, and hence any participant, individual or collective, is subject to the operation of its hegemony. As Jeffrey Juris and Alex Khasnabish (2013, 12–13) point out, 'networks are also associated with imperial domination, repression, and informational capitalism'; they are the new mechanisms of control that have replaced the hierarchical instruments of the Fordist period (Pugh 2011, 294).[5] If so, then the problem with accounts underlining benefits of 'connective action' (Bennett and Segerberg 2012) is that they fail to recognize the deliberate structuring that is intrinsic in the very tools that mediate activist communication today. With regard to specific platforms, such as Facebook, Twitter and so on, they 'do not come from out of nowhere' but have been designed and are controlled by powerful Internet corporations (Dolata and Schrape 2016, 7).[6] In short, naïve discourses of technology fail to recognize that networks themselves are a double-edged sword which empowers the capitalist elites at least as much as the activists themselves. In consequence, the discourse of networking may have contributed to narrowing of the activists' awareness of the mechanisms of capitalist oppression (Wolfson and Funke 2017) while, at the same time, having been successfully appropriated by neoliberalism for its own purposes (Leitner and Sheppard 2002).

Of the qualities assumed to be inherent in networks and hence in anti-neoliberal resistance, none received as much attention as horizontality. The idea that 'networking means no center, thus no central authority' (Castells 2010b, 156) is particularly important to various autonomist and neoanarchist positions that have been among the foremost intellectual influences on the alter-globalization movement. The anarchist writer Hakim Bey (2003, 107) thus exalts about 'the alternate horizontal open structure of info-exchange', and Hardt and Negri (2004, xiv) speak of the Multitude (the new revolutionary subject) as 'an open and expansive network in which all differences can be experienced freely and equally'. New social movements, argue Hardt and Negri (2012, 107), 'are powerful not despite their lack of leaders but because of it. They are organized horizontally as multitudes, and their insistence on democracy at all levels is more than a virtue but a key to their power'. For even more emphasis on horizontality, a post-development scholar and theorist of 'anti-globalization', Arturo Escobar, uses the jargon of 'meshworks', rather than networks (following Manuel de Landa). In cyberspace, Escobar argues, 'we find a viable and at least potentially meaningful model of social life' which is based on 'self-organisation and non-hierarchy' (Escobar 2009, 398). Overall, however, terminology is quite consistent across the literature about the technological dimension of anti-neoliberal activism with more recent accounts following a logic that is akin to the one popular a decade or more ago: 'Networks create spaces where individuals are free from hierarchical control structures. . . . This freedom is connected to the network structure of social media imitated in the Occupy movement' (Jones 2014, 160).

Like the claim to uniqueness, the assertion to horizontality is also highly problematic. The idea that networks are inherently antithetical to hierarchies may have promoted hidden, and thus potentially more dangerous and pervasive, inequalities of power within anti-neoliberal movements themselves; as a number of scholars have noted, the 'tyranny of structurelessness' (Freeman 1972) persists in contemporary activism (Dean 2009, 30; Halvorsen 2012, 430; Juris 2008, 17–18; Wolfson and Funke 2017). The thorny question of power in anti-neoliberal movements will be discussed in depth in chapter 4 which examines prefigurative politics and the related refusal by activists to implement any formal mechanisms of leadership while not acknowledging the endurance of informal ones. However, of particular relevance to questions of power in technologically enabled social movements is their particular mode of operation that Gerbaudo (2012, 139, emphasis in original) puts in the following, eloquent, way:

> *It is communication that organises, rather than organisation that communicates.* As a corollary, 'communicators' also automatically become 'organizers', given the influence they can have through their communications on the unfolding of collective action.

It follows that the claim to horizontality in movements revolving around platforms of social networking is not sustainable as communication in such networks is controlled by a small number of most committed and skilled activists or 'superactivists' (Gerbaudo 2012, 134–57; Van Laer 2010). Furthermore, while the Internet entails stratification among activists within movement networks, it also creates a digital divide between the networked activists and those who, for whichever reason, do not have access to the Internet or do not have a Facebook account. On a more symbolic level, technology may also cause a kind of semantic segregation based on the endogamous language and way of thinking that it engenders. As any reflective user of Facebook will realize, the platform tends to limit participants' exposure to views and vernaculars contradicting their own opinions and lifestyles. That is because content on Facebook is generated by and circulates among people who are usually already acquainted in one way or another and hence somewhat similar. A possible consequence of this is that 'virtual communities' become more and more secluded and internally increasingly homogenous, and so social pluralism turns out to be a mere slogan.

The foregoing discussion indicates that optimistic techno-centric determinism that is inherent in significant segments of anti-neoliberal theory and practice has not been left unchallenged. Its main claims are increasingly questioned by a literature that is growing in volume and sophistication and the relevance of which has been heightened by a parallel shift in activists' attention – away from cyberspace, as the predominant area of action, and towards real places. However, while some discursive by-products of anti-neoliberal activism's technological fixation, such as its claims to uniqueness and horizontality, have received polemical rejoinders, ideology – if mentioned at all – has not been in the centre of such critical accounts. This chapter now turns to unpacking important connections between fallacies of techno-centrism and the disavowal of ideology in the context of anti-neoliberal struggles.

REVOLUTION WITHOUT POLITICS?

> Today we invoke the word as if it were a discrete entity and thus a caus-
> ative factor – if not the chief causal factor – in every conceivable develop-
> ment of modernity. . . . Because of its peculiar susceptibility to reification,
> to being endowed with the magical power of an autonomous entity,
> technology is a major contributant to that gathering sense . . . of political
> impotence. The popularity of the belief that technology is the primary
> force shaping the postmodern world is a measure of our . . . neglect of
> moral and political standards, in making decisive choices about the direc-
> tion of society. (Marx 2001, 42)

The tendency to define activism in terms of the technologies that it uses rather than in relation to its underlying ideological vision is evident in some leading arguments concerning anti-neoliberal movements. Thus, for example, social anthropologist and activist Jeffrey Juris (2008, 15) maintains that 'expanding and diversifying networks is more than a concrete organisational objective; it is also a highly valued political goal'. According to Juris, networking is not a mere method of action but an emerging 'widespread cultural ideal' and 'a model for reorganizing society as a whole'. Similar reasoning is followed by another leading voice in the debate, the anarchist writer David Graeber (2002, 70) when he asserts that the movement 'is about creating and enacting horizontal networks' and 'these new forms of organization *are* its ideology' (emphasis in original).

As organizational logic networking is actually a topic with long history in anarchist thought,[7] the claim to a radical conceptual innovation that is com-monplace in discourses of contemporary activism can thus be put into some doubt. More generally, the inflated sense of radical novelty typical among many anti-neoliberals often serves to justify their inclination to ignore long-established traditions of progressive politics. Former political struggles and concomitant strategies and ideas are often a priori assumed to already be in the dustbin of history and to have nothing to offer to technologically empow-ered activists of today. To assert that 'the network has allowed humans to rebel' (Mason 2016, 24) is to unduly diminish the significance of the long history of resistance against oppression and exploitation. The struggles of the past were fought without network technology and yet, armed with ideas and courage of their militants, they achieved fundamental social changes and rights that we now take for granted. What is perhaps a natural human ten-dency – to overstate the significance of present-day events and developments – must not encourage a complete disregard for the past; yet, that is what lin-gers in accounts of contemporary activism written by technology evangelists.

Fixation with the ICT, so typical in anti-neoliberal discourses, entails neglect of the political purpose of activism and of the vision to underpin it. Technological tools of action tend to be reified as the causative agents and organizers of the mobilization, if not the very object of activism – as when the proclaimed goal of networked activism is to promote networking. In effect, as *The New Yorker*'s author Malcolm Gladwell writes in his critical essay on why 'the Revolution will not be tweeted', 'where activists were once defined by their causes, they are now defined by their tools' (Gladwell 2010). As I have already argued, parallel to the chronocentric underappreciation of history by many movement activists and intellectuals, and stemming from their limited interest in political economy, is their misperception of the context in which the ICT operates, namely their failure to recognize the degree of its penetration by hegemonic interests and ideology. Yet again, anti-neoliberal activists and writers unwittingly endorse the neoliberal vision of human nature. As Gerbaudo (2012, 8–9) puts it: 'The technovisionary discourse on social media appears as the reflection of a neoliberal ideology, incapable of understanding collective action except as the result of some sort of technological miracle fleetingly binding together egotistical individuals'.

Resulting from the broad misconception about the way how the ICT operates in the capitalist setting are more specific problems affecting the movements' political identities and strategies. The networked organizational forms that many activists and commentators are so enthused about have typically been represented as the overriding 'ideological' principle of the dissent which renders conventional ideological distinctions irrelevant (Graeber 2002, 70; 2004, 84; see also Bennett 2004, 118). According to such interpretations, the networking logic provides the means to unite diverse types of resistance to the neoliberal form of globalization by converging on one 'no' (Kingsnorth 2003) within the 'movement of movements' (Hardt 2002; Mertes 2004) or 'coalition of coalitions' (Klein 2001, 81; see also Dissent! 2005; Notes from Nowhere 2003; One-Off Press 2001; Shepard and Hayduk 2002; Starr 2000). Overlaps in organization and tactics between a plethora of different campaigns have been brought up as evidence that a broad and inclusive movement against neoliberalism is possible (see Jensen and Bang 2013 for a more recent example of this kind of reasoning). However, the notion that networking allows a radical diversity of voices to come together in action in spite of the significant differences in their respective world views is based on confused, if well-meaning, motives. This literature has been influenced by the enthusiasm associated with the scale and media impact of worldwide anti-neoliberal protests in the 1990s, particularly in Seattle in 1996, the symbolic resonance of the Zapatista uprising, and the esteem of Social Forums on regional and global scales. Riding on the wave of the political passion that these developments and events have engendered, authors writing about anti-neoliberal movements from an insider or sympathetic perspectives have tended to gloss over any potential impediment to the goal of large-scale net-worked mobilization against the neoliberal state and market. In this context, ideological diversity of the sundry enemies of neoliberalism has proven a conundrum. As both internal (postmodernism, politics of identity) and exter-nal (the discursive hegemony of neoliberalism) factors had already pushed discussions in terms of ideology out of political fashion, much of the early lit-erature on anti-neoliberal activism ended up dismissing ideology altogether. When 'the movement' was not described as outrightly 'post-ideological', then ideological differences were presented as simply surpassable in politi-cal practice – through the means of activist networking. At the same time, ideology itself continued to be presented as 'frozen and prescriptive', with a tendency 'to divide and exclude, rather than include and increase diversity' (Flesher Fominaya 2014, 69–70).

The alleged liberation from the ideological straitjacket was to be politi-cally empowering, but the problems that the claim has posed to progressive anti-neoliberalism in terms of its political identity continue to cause concern to activists and sympathetic scholars alike. For example, attempts to capture this miscellaneous range of ideological projects in terms of one broad politics of opposition, or 'one world with many worlds in it' (Klein 2001, 89), have led to political as well as conceptual controversies that have permeated 'the movement'. Thus, in the 1990s and early 2000s the opponents of the neolib-eral form of globalization were often described as 'anti-globalists' causing unease among Marxist and other internationalist critics who rejected the label of 'anti-globalization' as opening them to charges of isolationism. Con-versely, appellations such as 'globalization-from-below' or the 'global justice movement' were applied in an insufficiently discerning manner to a huge variety of positions, some of which did not identify with any global agenda. More problematically, an unwarranted 'ecumenism' relating to political val-ues and belief systems has become a norm in the literature on activism. The tendency is described accurately by Jeremy Gilbert (2008, 205):

> The standard form which the literature of the movement takes is what we might call the anti-capitalist catalogue: a gazetteer surveying of a disparate range of current organisations, movements and campaigns, with often no direct and very little indirect links between them beyond the imaginative assertions of their chroniclers that they do indeed add up to some kind of large-scale movement.[8]

Incongruous registers of mutually contradictory positions are intellectually problematic. But more thorny *political* implications may also stem from the assumption that, thanks to the networking opportunities afforded by the

ICT, there is now room for an all-encompassing front against neoliberalism.[9] The idea has led some academics and insiders (to the dismay of others) to advocate alliances between fundamentally different perspectives such as right-wing separatism and anarchism (Starr n.d.), a suggestion that has had some rather negative consequences for the public image of a putative progressive counter-hegemonic project as well as causing considerable uneasiness among commentators on the left (see, e.g., Amin 2011, 191–92; Anton 2007, 27; Berlet and Lyons 2000, 342–43; Pressebüro Savanne 2000; Sakai 2003). Similar concerns have been raised with regard to the inchoate and contradictory nature of more recent activist mobilizations, such as the Occupy: 'The atrophy of the left during 40 years of neoliberal hegemony . . . has resulted in an uncritical optimism and historical amnesia of the potentially deeply reactionary forms such amorphous discontent might take' (Taylor 2013, 743; see also Brass 2014, 253). I will return to this problem in the discussion of the 99 percent discourse in chapter 5.

It is thus clear that while the benefits of the ICT are enormous, problems also abound regarding its impact on activism, or – more precisely – regarding the way how it has been reified, if not idolized, in some influential interpretations. The reification of technology has led to illusions within anti-neoliberal politics, for example, the fantasies of exceptionality and horizontality, that increased the movements' susceptibility to operations of neoliberal hegemony. The obsession with the ICT, and the associated chronocentric assumption of the overall uniqueness of the current era, has also left activists unprepared, or unwilling, to appreciate the ideational resources obtainable from the history of past political mobilizations.

At the same time, a question that begs an answer pertains to the effectiveness of the strategies and approaches preferred by anti-neoliberal movements today. After all, it could be argued that if the movements are successful, then questions of the activists' awareness or otherwise – of ideology, history, the nature of the political context in which their preferred technologies operate and so on – is of secondary significance. Alas, as I will have more occasions to show, even according to most sympathetic evaluations, the movements' achievements have been disappointing, particularly considering that the recent destabilization of the neoliberal system provided its progressive challengers with great political opportunities that they, by and large, have not seized.

Of course, to isolate technology as the primary cause of the underwhelming track record of anti-neoliberal activism would be a mistake mirroring the reification of technology typical of the techno-enthusiastic interpretations. But it is not controversial to say that, among other factors, technological tools tend to structure political activism in certain ways, and a number of scholars have focused on this matter and specifically on the effectiveness of political action online. While some authors stress a promising potential of 'flash flood' political activism (Earl et al. 2015) caused by 'loosely (and even temporarily) engaged participants' (356), others have described mass online campaigning as 'slacktivism'. Its power to enact a durable political change has been questioned by critics such as Morozov (2009a), who described it as a 'feel good activism that has zero political or social impact', or Gladwell, who highlighted that it is built around weak ties suitable for quick mass mobilization on narrow issues but precluding commitment necessary to bring about a more comprehensive social change. As Gladwell (2010) says, ICT 'makes it easier for activists to express themselves, and harder for that expression to have any impact'. Fixation with technologically mediated action leaves activists susceptible to what Jodi Dean (2009, 17–18, 32–33) calls *technological fetishism*, that is to say, an illusion of political participation and impact through the modern media of communication. Dean's point resonates with Gladwell's: The mere circulation of electronic content, however politicized, by activists and 'the academic and typing left' (Dean 2009) does not, in itself, lead to meaningful political outcomes. In the absence of critical reflection by activists who have neglected other ways of making political strides, these technologies, or rather, the ways their impact has been absorbed, have contributed to the movements' failings. A case in point is discussed by Gerbaudo (2012, 69) in his account of the effects of technology in the authoritarian context of the Arab Spring. Gerbaudo reports how the decision of the Egyptian authorities to shut the Internet down actually strengthened the protest; the shutdown 'made it impossible to maintain a safe distance by following events on the internet or talking on the phone to one's friends on the streets. . . . To get even a glimpse of what was going on, one had to take to the streets' (69).

The last point relates to anti-neoliberal activism's evolution in recent years, with its attention directed increasingly towards making a political statement through action in urban space – a shift, in Gerbaudo's terms, from 'the tweets' to 'the streets'.[10] As the activists associated with the *Indignados* movement, and then Occupy, exclaimed, 'we are not on Facebook, we are on the street!' (Gerbaudo 2012, 76–101; see also Halvorsen 2012; McCurdy, Feigenbaum and Frenzel 2016). This insistence on reclaiming the public space may be a sign that activists have started to recognize the limitations as well as opportunities associated with networking. In light of the argument presented in this chapter this would be a positive development. However, as I will argue next, while the repertoire of political measures has been enriched by the strategy of occupation of public squares, the focus of activist discourses and narratives has remained on the means of action rather than its ends. Of course, the latter inform the former and so cannot be separated; ideologies are as much about visions of the ideal world as about the best ways of getting there. But insistence on a 'prefigurative' way of doing politics, where the ideal is to be enacted primarily in what activists do in their daily running of the movement, has not been accompanied by proper consideration of the answer to the fundamental question: 'What do we want?'. Indeed, some branches of anti-neoliberalism have refused to pose the question in the first place, preferring to indulge in the experience of activism itself. Chapter 4 turns to prefiguration as another idea in the centre of anti-neoliberal discourses and practices and several problems that it has posed, in the absence of a systematic ideological deliberation, to the dominant forms of anti-neoliberal activism today.

NOTES

1. In crude terms, the evolution of the Internet consists of two stages: Web 1.0 and Web 2.0. They overlap in some respects, as Web 1.0 did not disappear entirely with the arrival of Web 2.0, but are broadly distinguishable based on the differences in speed (telephone dial-up versus high-speed connections), access (stationary computers versus mobile devices accessible on the go) and content (provider-generated versus user-generated). There is also some preliminary discussion of Web 3.0 which is currently under construction.

2. Castells 2010b, especially 71–167, and Juris 2008 are among the most influential scholarly accounts that emphasize the salience of networks.

3. This is not to downplay the role of social networking in making the international public aware of what was going on in Iran and, later, in Egypt and elsewhere during the Arab Spring.

4. Symptomatically, the notion of technological empowerment of ordinary people against oppressive regimes was also keenly endorsed by shakers and movers of the ICT industry, including Mark Zuckerberg who was convinced of Facebook's destiny to fulfil a fundamental role in the process of global democratization. In a letter to potential investors Zuckerberg (2012) wrote: 'We hope to change how people relate to their governments and social institutions. . . . By giving people the power to share, we are starting to see people make their voices heard on a different scale from what has historically been possible. These voices will increase in number and volume. They cannot be ignored'.

5. Scholars such as Morozov (2011) also argue that social networking media can serve as very effective platforms for governmental surveillance and hence pose a real danger to activists.

6. It should also be noted that Facebook or Twitter are primarily tools for individual self-promotion, while much of the user-generated content is then appropriated by capitalist interests controlling the cyberspace: 'The Internet does not transcend global capitalism but is deeply involved with it by virtue of the corporate interests it supports and the discourses of capitalism and neoliberalism that the people who use it are drenched in' (Fenton and Barassi 2011, 192–93).

7. This fact is acknowledged by Juris (2008, 10, 86; see also Flesher Fominaya 2014, 74) but is not usually highlighted in the literature on anti-neoliberal movements.

8. An example of this tendency is a book on resistance to neoliberal globalization written by Charles Lindholm and José Pedro Zúquete (2010). Although Lindholm and Zúquete declare appreciation of ideological plurality, their argument actually envisages diverse ideological positions as sharing 'a *grand narrative* based on a "common ethical core and a common mental map" that has arisen in response to globalization' (2010, 10). However, since the perspectives discussed by Lindholm and Zúquete include the European fascist 'New Right' network, Hugo Chavez's socialist populism, the ideological kit of the Zapatistas, the militant discourse of Al Qaeda and diverse ideas associated with the politics of the World Social Forum, it is difficult to see what they could share except, perhaps, for networking (in terms of their mode of operation) and their hostility to the disembedding forces of neoliberal globalization, a common ground so ideologically thin that it does not provide any meaningful basis for collective action.

9. Interestingly, writers hypothesizing a transcendence of ideological divisions in the political praxis of 'the movement' may end up disparaging inconvenient ideological positions. A case in point is Marianne Maeckelbergh, whose book declares at the outset 'to understand the diverse practices and beliefs of the alterglobalisation movement as a single movement because part of the political project outlined here is precisely to overcome the assumption that difference precludes unity' (2009, 6). Maeckelbergh then goes on to list 'the most important political values, structures and practices of the alterglobalisation movement' (2009, 8), most of which relate to the dynamics of 'the movement' itself rather than any broader political vision beyond autotelic participation. But, although steadfast in her belief that 'the movement' is capable of overcoming its cleavages, Maeckelbergh associates it primarily with anarchism while seeming rather disdainful of a far left position within it that advocates the need to move beyond the mere preoccupation with the political process itself (2009, 76). This is an example of how proponents of an all-inclusive unity of 'the movement' ironically end up implying that inconvenient elements do not, in some respects at least, fit in there. Of course, what such assertions inadvertently reveal is that ideological identities are not just a matter of academic interest. Ideological labels may be empowering when they are seen as linked with momentous intellectual achievements or decisive, positively valued, political events. Alternatively, they may be disabling when they are associated with negative contexts. How those contexts are interpreted in any given instance will obviously depend on the ideological perspective in question. What is empowering for one ideology may be seen as delegitimizing from a different ideological angle. Any instance of discursive contestation of neoliberalism is dependent on the broader ideology that it inevitably inhabits and, therefore, heated controversies on, for example, the best way to challenge neoliberalism abound along the fluctuating, but nonetheless identifiable, divisions between major ideological families (Soborski 2007, 2013).

10. The words of a Marxist scholar, David Harvey (2012, 161–62), resonate with this phrase: 'The collective power of bodies in public space is still the most effective instrument of opposition. . . . It is bodies on the street and in the squares, not the babble of sentiments on Twitter and Facebook, that really matter'.

Chapter 4

The Charms and Traps of Prefigurative Politics

Prefiguration is at the heart of anti-neoliberal activism. The intention of a prefigurative action is to unite its means with its aims; in other words, in a prefigurative movement the process is harmonized with the objective. The appeal of prefiguration is related to a widespread perception that corruption and hypocrisy are all-pervasive in mainstream political space. However, this model of activism has some important flaws. Thus, prefigurative commitment to horizontal organizing has obfuscated the entrenched mechanisms of informal power in operation within anti-neoliberal movements while at the same time hindering the movements' effectiveness. Further setbacks stem from the fact that prefigurative politics typical of anti-neoliberalism has a highly individualistic dimension and so is fairly compatible with aspects of the neoliberal vision of human nature, especially its preoccupation with personal autonomy. Insistence on prefigurative principles has also led to a substitution of quarrels about the logistics of activism for any systematic debate about its political vision or purpose. This chapter maps some of the main controversies surrounding prefiguration and brings the question of ideology into the debate about its implications.

PREFIGURATION: HISTORY AND CONCEPTUAL CONNECTIONS

All human experience teaches that methods and means cannot be separated from the ultimate aim. The means employed become, through individual habit and social practice, part and parcel of the final purpose; they influence it, modify it, and presently the aims and means become identical. (Goldman 2005 [1924])

Prefigurative politics has been advocated for, and debated within, anti-neoliberal activism at different points in its evolution including alter-globalist movements of the 1990s, World Social Forums and, especially, recent mobilizations, such as *Indignados* and Occupy. But while prefiguration is an integral aspect of much of contemporary activism both in the Global North and South – it has, for example, shaped some forms of resistance in Latin America (Sader 2008) and recent protests in the Arab World (Bayat 2013) – prefigurative ideas and practices long predate today's movements and campaigns.

Carl Boggs is credited with the invention of the term 'prefiguration' which he used in relation to various revolutionary movements, primarily in Russia, Germany, Italy and Spain as well as the American New Left. In Boggs's writing (1977/1978, 100), prefigurative politics stands for 'the embodiment, within the ongoing political practice of a movement, of those forms of social relations, decision-making, culture, and human experience that are the ultimate goal'. Prefigurative practices, thus understood, can be traced back to nineteenth-century socialist communes that aimed to enact the kind of society that was desired by utopian socialists such as Charles Fourier. The ideal of collapsing the distinction between means and ends of political action has also been a major characteristic of anarchism: In fact, it is clearly identifiable in works by classical anarchist thinkers, including Emma Goldman (quoted earlier) and James Guillaume, a friend and follower of Bakunin, who articulated the idea in simple terms: 'How could one want an equalitarian and free society to issue from authoritarian organisation? It is impossible' (in Franks 2010, 145). Prefigurative sensibilities are also evident in the programme of the Industrial Workers of the World, an international workers union established in 1905, whose Constitution (in the Preamble) declares the goal of the organization to be 'forming the structure of the new society within the shell of the old' (IWW 2002 [1905]). Likewise, Mohandas Gandhi's belief that 'if we could change ourselves, the tendencies in the world would also change' (often popularized as 'be the change you wish to see in the world') resonates with the notion of prefiguration (in Davis and Harrison 2013, 171). A prefigurative approach was also practiced by the 1960s New Left organization Students for a Democratic Society (Breines 1989) and, from 1971 to 1988, by the US-based Movement for a New Society, a network bringing together radical pacifists and feminists (Cornell 2009).

In light of this telegraphic summary, to which many more examples could be added, it is inaccurate to claim, as some contemporary advocates of prefigurative approach have done, that prefiguration renders anti-neoliberal activism 'different from previous movements' (Maeckelbergh 2011, 3). Prefiguration has a long history, and it is perhaps unfortunate that many of its exponents and practitioners today, convinced of own uniqueness, are disinclined to acknowledge its past and learn from it. Part of my argument here is that, in contrast to what prefigurative methods meant to encourage previously, namely consistency between a political vision and the path towards its realization, the idea is now invoked predominantly to justify a refusal to endorse any clear political goal and a substitution for it of an autotelic celebration of the experience of activism itself. As I noted in earlier parts of this book, anti-neoliberal activism consists of many diverse strands with distinctive, albeit usually unacknowledged, ideological identities. Prefiguration, as both a concept and a practice, is particularly popular in movements that can be classified as anarchist (Bray 2013). However, such a characterization draws on their merely selective and pragmatic adoption of ideas that have an anarchist lineage (Rohgalf 2013, 161–62). In other words, these movements are described as anarchist 'mainly out of temperamental reflex, not rigorous thought' (Featherstone, Henwood and Parenti n.d.). Therefore, their prefigurative commitments are not usually anchored in a firm theoretical foundation. Indeed, political theory is typically seen as having no application in prefigurative activism, and a strong link is often drawn between the practice of prefiguration and the ostensible absence of ideology; accordingly, prefiguration allows activists to 'generate possibilities without imposing ideologies' (Harcourt 2012, 35). In other words:

> What matters is the process, more than the product. In fact, the process is the product. . . . . New society will result from the process, not from a preconceived blueprint of what the product should be. This is the true revolutionary transformation: the material production of social change not from programmatic goals but from the networked experiences of the actors in the movement. (Castells 2015, 147)

In anti-neoliberal discourses of an anarchist ilk, prefiguration is connected with ideas of horizontality, direct democracy, autonomy, creativity and spontaneity. One of the reasons why ideology tends to be renounced by activists is its association, in activist thinking, with hierarchical and dogmatic organizations and hence its incongruity with the idea of horizontality. At the same time, ideology's alleged rigidity means it is also rejected as incompatible with a pursuit of creativity and individual autonomy of movement participants. Even though the word 'ideology' is not necessarily used in such arguments, prefiguration is typically contrasted with political programmes and blueprints or, indeed, any preconceived objectives, and these, in turn, tend to be viewed as part and parcel of the ideological domain.

It is thus in juxtaposition with what ideology has often been reduced to in such arguments, namely hierarchical political organizations and their inflexible doctrines and policy proposals, that the charm of prefiguration seems particularly alluring to contemporary activists. However, the problem with this way of thinking about prefiguration is that the principles that are to be prefigured in political action tend to be rejoiced for the dynamics that they generate within the space of activism rather than for any impact they might have on the broader world. In other words, while the mode of operation, or the 'how' of the movement, is in the centre of the activists' self-reflection, the purpose of it – the 'what for' – is not given adequate attention. At the same time, as a number of critics have pointed out, the politics of prefiguration 'tends to hinder . . . fruitful social analyses and political struggles' (Rohgalf 2013, 153) and 'precludes a politics beyond the tautology "we don't like the present situation"' (Brass 2014, 255).

While prefiguration promises to liberate activists from the straitjacket of political organization and doctrine, it also carries with it the risk of withdrawal 'into a hedonistic experience of activism' (Pleyers 2010, 99) and of 'fetishization of form over function' (Wolfson and Funke 2017, 90) or, in another turn of phrase, a 'fusion of form and content that reduces the latter to the former' (Taylor 2013, 738). In the process, the movement becomes both too close to its enemy, as prefigurative principles cohere with neoliberalism's affirmed adherence to values of creativity and autonomy, and too distant from the public, as outsiders, in particular individuals from more disadvantaged social strata, often do not feel welcome in the spaces of prefiguration (Juris 2013, 57). There is a degree of truth in the opinion, advanced by some mainstream observers, that the most recent eruption of protest against neoliberalism – namely Occupy, an activist mobilization with prefiguration at its very centre – 'was an insular movement, whose members spoke mainly to each other' (Nocera 2012). The rest of this chapter focuses on some key concepts that are connected to the idea of prefiguration in anti-neoliberal discourses, especially horizontality, autonomy and spontaneity – and examines the main intellectual and strategic weaknesses afflicting anti-neoliberal movements due to their prefigurative methodology and in the concomitant absence of an explicit ideological reflection.

THE HERE AND NOW OF PREFIGURATION

> They harvested themselves. They harvested the salt of the earth. And they became free. (Castells 2015, 201)

In chapter 3, I discussed the activist celebration of networking as an operative mode that is assumed conducive for horizontality, a principle with utmost significance for many progressive anti-neoliberal movements. Horizontality and the associated ideas of direct democracy and consensus decision-making are also at the centre of arguments about prefiguration. In fact, some authors conflate generic and specifically anti-neoliberal connotations of the term and thus equate 'prefigurative' with 'horizontal' politics:

> Prefigurative politics denotes a politics that is based on horizontal, autonomous and leaderless forms of self-organising and struggle. Its aim is to prefigure the world we want to live in in the here and now of the ways in which social movements and autonomous groups govern themselves and organise actions. (Szolucha 2013, 22)

Horizontalism (a political attitude favouring non-hierarchical political arrangements) has been a key feature of many instances of anti-neoliberal organizing. For example, while the Zapatista movement is, out of necessity, vertically structured (as Zapatista Army of National Liberation), it inspired the creation, in 1996, of the People's Global Action, a network that places a lot of emphasis on horizontal arrangements of its political processes and that has been of major significance to the evolution of the global justice movement. The preoccupation with horizontality typical of some currents of the latter form of alter-globalism has then fed – via Argentine *piquetero* movement in the wake of the country's 2001 economic crisis (Sitrin 2011) – into recent mobilizations of resistance, including the Arab Spring, *Indignados* and Occupy. However, horizontalism has a much longer history: Sitrin (2011) notes its early instances in ancient Greece and in Native American systems of justice; it was also a key attribute of New Left movements in the 1960s and 1970s.

Anti-neoliberal advocates of horizontality applaud its alleged prevalence in contemporary forms of protest and resistance. For Graeber (2002, 70), activism is 'about creating and enacting horizontal networks . . . based on principles of decentralized, nonhierarchical consensus democracy'. Hardt and Negri insist that anti-neoliberal movements rely on 'swarm intelligence' (2004, 91–93) and 'are powerful not despite their lack of leaders but because of it. . . . Their insistence on democracy at all levels is more than a virtue but a key to their power' (2012, 107). Castells (2015, 82), in his discussion of Occupy, maintains that, 'there was no traditional leadership, no rational leadership and no charismatic leadership . . . and certainly no personalized leadership' in the movement. The Arab Spring was also described as a horizontal mobilization: 'the fact that the uprising was leaderless meant that everyone was a leader – and this meant an immeasurable sense of personal empowerment' (Fernández-Savater and Flesher Fominaya 2017, 145). The 'horizontal social articulation' (Whitaker 2009, 82) of anti-neoliberal activism implies an unequivocal rejection of organizations such as the state, the party, or the trade union, in favour of a radically participatory method, where decision-making is not delegated but a shared responsibility of every movement participant. Current debates over horizontality and direct democracy and the practicing of these principles in anti-neoliberal activism revolve around two foci: World Social Forum (WSF) and, in particular, the Occupy movement and other instances of protest encampments following the 2007–2008 financial crisis.

The WSF is an annual meeting of civil society groups but defines itself as 'a permanent process of seeking and building alternatives which cannot be reduced to the events supporting it'. The WSF 'belongs' only to social movements, that is to say, it is closed to political parties. It attempts to prevent authority from crystallizing within its processes by declaring that no movement can speak on behalf of the Forum which 'does not constitute a locus of power to be disputed by the participants' (WSF 2001). The horizontal nature of the WSF is also asserted by its prominent advocates. For example, one of its founders, a Brazilian architect, politician and social activist, Chico Whitaker (2009, 83, 82) describes the WSF as a '*horizontal space*' with '*no leaders*' or 'public *square without an owner*' and commends the power of its 'open, free, horizontal structures' (emphasis in original). However, the degree of horizontality of the WSF has been put into some doubt by a number of commentators as well as some insiders who brought up the question of 'tension between aspirations and practices' in the WSF (Caruso 2013, 81). The critiques focused on the 'star' system that has dominated the Forum, and the informal authority acquired by 'social movement entrepreneurs' (Rigon 2015, 81–82), namely individuals with relevant traits and skills, such as proficiency in public speaking or just the knowledge of English which is the Forum's language of communication (Caruso 2013, 81–82). Others highlighted gender as a major factor influencing power dynamics within the space of the Forum (Conway 2011). As the WSF developed, critics of the horizontality claim had increasingly more ammunition available to back up their counter-arguments. It was already the first WSF (in 2001) that was sponsored by a political party (the Brazilian Workers Party) and so, in spite of its declared prefigurative rejection of mainstream political organizations, inevitably became an actor in Brazil's electoral contest at that time. Later, to the dismay of some participants and commentators, commercial interests began to exert their influence as well by supporting the WSF financially. Critics were particularly suspicious of the sponsorship of several editions of the Forum by the Ford Foundation alongside a number of other corporate entities closely associated with neoliberal agenda (Chossudovsky 2016). The WSF was also dismissed by some as a non-governmental organization fair, particularly the 2007 Forum in Nairobi (Manji 2007) – the latter was additionally disparaged for its prohibitively high costs that made it impossible for many local activists to attend (Ma'anit 2007). The problem with access was stated boldly by Teivo Teivainen (2008, 4): 'To claim that the WSF is an "open space" may sound like a joke in bad taste for those who do not have the material means to enter the space'.

While the Forum's horizontal nature continues to be a highly contested matter, it is with regard to the Occupy movement that the debate about horizontality became particularly intense. In Occupy's case, the principle was linked to consensus decision-making that Occupiers carried out in a way that resembled direct democracy practices in earlier progressive movements and often repeated their flaws (Polletta 2002; Smith and Glidden 2012). Consensus is associated especially with Quaker communities where it has been used fairly effectively, but it proves highly problematic in a setting like Occupy which brought together a huge diversity of participants, many of them with highly individualistic identities.[1] In other words, consensus decision-making may work in groups whose members share values (as is, broadly speaking, the situation with Quakers). But in a 'movement' defined by agenda as wide-ranging and diverse as anti-neoliberalism, consensus proves counter-productive as it can only be achieved at the cost of diluting the matters down to the level of generality acceptable to everybody involved.[2]

Indeed, as it happens, the Occupy movement, which claimed to represent 99 percent of the population, and whose 'demands [were] multiple and motivations unlimited' (Castells 2015, 255), marked a climax of programmatic vagueness as far as anti-neoliberal activism is concerned. This is an issue that requires a more extensive discussion (which will be offered in chapter 5), but what should be clear at this point is that it was simply impossible to agree on goals that every occupier could endorse. Initially, the mobilization was to be about 'one demand' so broad and obvious that everyone in Occupy would support it; that is, at least, what the original call-for-action poster, designed by *Adbusters* magazine, implied. The poster featured a ballerina dancing on the bronze statue of a charging bull which is situated near Wall Street. Above the ballerina, there is the caption 'WHAT IS OUR ONE DEMAND?', while at the bottom of the poster is the hashtag #OCCUPY WALL STREET. Yet the quest for even this one demand was soon abandoned: In a movement so diverse and so fixated on absolute democracy an agreement on what the demand was to be proved impossible to reach. As Rodrigo Nunes explains: 'The dream of "absolute openness" means that openness is only possible if we abstract all concrete differences. Also, nothing can ever be affirmed, for that would contradict openness' (Nunes 2005, 311). In effect, since any single demand would have been too restrictive and divisive, Occupy ended up being a movement 'with no demands', and many activists and fellow travellers assumed that this, and the associated slogan of the movement – 'We Are Our Demands' – represented radicalism at its purest.

It is a potentially discomforting question, in the context of all this pre-figurative effort, whether Occupy was in fact as genuinely horizontal as it declared itself to be. As with the WSF, some commentators are not convinced. For example, Pablo Gerbaudo (2012, 108) makes the following point apropos Occupy Wall Street (OWS) (while also advancing a similar argument regarding Arab Spring uprisings and the *Indignados* movement): 'Against the claims to spontaneity and leaderlessness which have since been associated with the movement, at its inception Occupy was a carefully orchestrated campaign'. Gerbaudo's is one of many accounts demonstrating that in OWS, in analogy to the situation in the WSF, an elite group of activists assumed the role of 'opinion' and 'organisational' leaders: 'Such activists came to acquire a role as invisible choreographers who by using social media to publicise the movement's plans and events have had much influence in shaping its manifestations' (2012, 131, 132). Other activists and scholars have reported that, as with the WSF, hierarchies based on gender, ethnicity and class were also discernible in various Occupy camps (Anonymous 2012; Grande 2013; Pickerill and Krinsky 2012).

Horizontality and leaderlessness claims can also be questioned using concepts that are well established in social sciences, such as Michels's 'iron law of oligarchy' (Scerri 2013), or in previous activist discussions. Of particular relevance is a phenomenon described by Jo Freeman (1972) as the 'tyranny of structurelessness'. Using 1960s' anarcho-feminist movements as her examples, Freeman argues that 'there is no such thing as a "structureless" group', because 'any group of people of whatever nature that comes together for any length of time for any purpose will inevitably structure itself in some fashion'. According to Freeman, while structurelessness is not possible to accomplish in social practice, the idea is also dangerous in that it obscures the operation of informal and unacknowledged mechanisms of power. In the absence of formal structures, a hidden, and hence intractable, system of power-making takes hold, based on celebrity status of some group members or their superior cultural capital. A major problem in this context is lack of accountability of such informal leaders: Since their leadership is not officially acknowledged, they are, ipso facto, not constrained by any proper limitations. As Freeman writes: 'If the movement continues deliberately not to select who shall exercise power, it does not thereby abolish power. All it does is abdicate the right to demand that those who do exercise power and influence be responsible for it'. Having witnessed the 'star system' informally materialized within feminist activism, Freeman insists that 'for everyone to have the opportunity to be involved in a given group and to participate in its activities the structure must be explicit, not implicit'. In a similar way, denial of leadership structures, today so frequently asserted by leading anti-neoliberal activists and fellow-travelling academics, actually serves, regardless of intentions, to render activism less democratic.

The recognition of the problem is on the increase in the literature on anti-neoliberal movements, and several authors have invoked Freeman's contribution when evaluating the impact of the horizontality claim on the real mechanisms of power in anti-neoliberal activism. The already mentioned analysis by Gerbaudo (2012, 36) makes the point that 'we have to be suspicious of interpretations . . . that view collective action as springing forth spontaneously, without the need for organisational mediation or symbolic articulation to shape and guide it'. He identifies in anti-neoliberal movements 'soft, indirect, and invisible . . . forms of leadership' (2012, 163). Similarly, Jan Rohgalf (2013, 161) argues, in relation to Occupy, that 'the power which is vigilantly dismantled at the front of the stage sneaks in unnoticed through the back-door – probably in the brutal guise of bullying, intimidation, and banishment' (Rohgalf 2013, 161).

While, in line with such critical accounts, horizontality is a fiction with detrimental consequences in terms of the movement's transparency and accountability, the activists' adherence to this notion has also, on several occasions, proven to be a significant barrier to their success. Again, Freeman's work provides insights into how activists' efforts may be impaired by the fantasy of structurelessness: 'If the movement continues to keep power as diffuse as possible . . . it simultaneously ensures that the movement is as ineffective as possible'. It is not hard to find illustrations of this predicament in recent anti-neoliberal mobilizations. For example, Jackie Smith and Bob Glidden (2012) discern problems caused by consensus practices in the case of Occupy Pittsburgh – namely, a paralysis of the decision-making process and a waste of energy that could have been used to build a stronger movement. Another case in point is provided by Occupy Denver. Its activists, in response to Denver Mayor's request to nominate a representative to speak and negotiate on their behalf, elected a three-year-old border collie, Shelby, as their leader (Huffington Post 2011). Of course, it remains a matter of speculation if they could have made any progress, and at what cost, by engaging with the city's authorities. On the other hand, a more tragic example of the possible implications of the horizontal and anti-institutional approach is what happened with the Gezi movement in Istanbul. The movement's refusal to put forward any formal representation led to its crushing by the Turkish government – the government was initially willing to talk, but there was nobody to talk to; in the meantime, the movement started eroding under the burden of its internal quarrels and so became an easy target for the repression by the police (Tufekci 2014, 14–15).

Relatedly to problems with the horizontality claim, another line of criticism of the prefigurative politics typical of anti-neoliberal activism draws attention to the implications of its highly individualistic disposition. For example, as far as Occupy is concerned, the movement revolved around its participants – 'We Are Our Demands' – but not as parts of a united collective

but as individuals whose identities were not to be 'oppressed' by a political programme or predetermined group commitments. The occupiers were
brought together by a shared occupation of a part of city space and a joint
engagement in a 'hedonistic experience of activism' (Pleyers 2010, 99) –
something akin, perhaps, to the rave gathering or drug experience (Srnicek
and Williams 2015, 7). There was deliberate absence of any clear purpose or
vision to unify the cacophony of voices celebrated in the space of occupation and certainly no structure that would extend the movement's existence
beyond the temporality of the occupation.

The individualistic nature of the majority of contemporary prefigurative
movements has led critics to denounce this form of activism as revolving
around 'ethical acts in themselves: personal statements of awareness, rather
than attempts to engage politically with society' (Chandler 2009, 78–79).
It has also been highlighted that, relatedly to its depoliticizing impact, the
idea of prefiguration seems compatible with some key aspects of the neoliberal vision of human nature and its prioritization of personal autonomy and
creativity (Pugh 2011, 294). At the same time, it has been noted, a typical
long-term expression of prefigurative commitments is often limited to ethical
consumerism (Dean 2009, 34). A classic work in this respect is the study of
the 'new spirit of capitalism' by French sociologists Luc Boltanski and Ève
Chiapello. They identify the following as the defining qualities of the new
capitalist system:

> Autonomy, spontaneity, rhizomorphous capacity, multitasking . . . convivial-
> ity, openness to others and novelty, availability, creativity, visionary intuition,
> sensitivity to differences, listening to lived experience and receptiveness to a
> whole range of experiences, being attracted to informality and the search for
> interpersonal contacts. (Boltanski and Chiapello 2007, 97)

The key argument in Boltanski and Chiapello's book is that the values of
the new capitalism discussed here 'are taken directly from the repertoire of
May 1968' (2007, 97). The overlap between counter-cultural and neoliberal
and consumerist values has been discussed extensively also in popular sociological and cultural studies books (e.g., Frank 1997; Heath and Potter 2006).
Nevertheless, the elective affinity between prefigurative activism, rooted as it
is in the New Left's political culture of the 1960s, and neoliberalism remains
largely unacknowledged by the academic enthusiasts as well as practitioners
of prefiguration.[3]

A related point to note is that prefigurative politics may have a class
dimension. As Juris (2013, 57) observes, it is preferred by middle-class
white youth, while working-class activists of colour do not feel welcome in
the spaces of this form of activism. While rituals –a facet of many types of

political action (Flood 2002, 182–194) but particularly significant in prefigurative movements – tend to have an energizing influence on their participants,
they can also 'be exclusive and define a subset of a movement against others
or become "mere" ritual that may be devoid of effective political content
beyond its performance' (Pickerill and Krinsky 2012, 284). Thus, as I noted
earlier with specific references to WSF and Occupy, divisions are still present; as per usual, the cherished principle of inclusivity is easier to declare than
accomplish. Implicit in these problems, and particularly apparent in recent
mobilizations such as Occupy, is that anti-neoliberal activists do not seem
explicitly committed to making any impact on the outside world with 'many
camps focusing more on the politics of camp life rather than the politics of the
action itself' (Pickerill and Krinsky 2012, 283). The concluding part of this
chapter focuses on how the practice of activism has been venerated in arguments celebrating prefigurative politics and brings to light the problematic
implications of the movements' self-absorption evident in such assertions.

PREFIGURATION AS EVASION

> The apparatus of general assemblies, human microphones, and hand sig-
> nals contribute, perhaps unwittingly, to the effort [to be leaderless]. The
> 'human mic', for instance – as a form of expression, communication,
> and amplification – has the effect of undermining leadership. The human
> mic interrupts charisma. It's like live translation; the speaker can only
> utter five to eight words before having to shut up, while the assembled
> masses repeat. The effect is to defuse oratory momentum – or to render it
> numbingly repetitive. It also forces the assembled masses to utter words
> and arguments that they may not agree with – which has the effect of
> slowing down political momentum and undermining the consolidation of
> leadership. . . . There are common hand signals with designated meanings.
> A triangular hand signal raises an issue of process. The rolling arms mean
> they've heard enough. Interventions need to be short. There is the possibil-
> ity of a block. The human mic controls. 'Mic check, mic check' – the 'mic
> check' becomes a command, an order, a call to attention. And the rules are
> enforced by the subtle pressure of the assembled group. (Harcourt 2012,
> 39–40, 42)

This lengthy quote is taken from a typical sympathetic account of how things
were run at Occupy Wall Street. The focus is on the facilitation of the assem-
bly and the measures to ensure that deliberations are organized in a way that
prefigures the values cherished by the occupiers. The author, an American
critical theorist, posits, with exaggeration typical of many enthusiasts of the
prefigurative approach, that the movement represents a 'new paradigm' and

'new political grammar' and that, among other factors that imbue it with novelty, it is also new on account of its non-ideological character: 'A leaderless occupation without demands: It is almost as if our language never caught up with this political phenomenon' (Harcourt 2012, 44). Harcourt's exemplifies the kind of argument that has prevailed in insiders' and fellow travellers' discussions of Occupy. The rituals involved in the daily operations of the mobilization are described in such accounts as epitomizing the principles of the movement, such as horizontality. Since one should not 'curtail the growing mystique of Occupy Wall Street with something as ordinary as a political demand' (Greenberg 2011) the movement turns out to be primarily about those very rituals, or the celebration of activism itself, rather than aiming to have any political effect on society at large.

Contrary to claims affirming Occupy's unprecedented qualities, the kind of attitude described by Harcourt and others is not new. The idea is present in Michel Foucault's writing, as Harcourt himself admits. 'It is not up to us to propose' – said Foucault – 'as soon as one "proposes" – one proposes a vocabulary, an ideology, which can only have effects of domination' (in Harcourt 2012, 39). Writing about ostensibly structureless anarcho-feminist movements of the 1960s, Freeman identified (reproachfully) a similar lack of purpose outside the activist space: 'The mere act of staying together becomes the reason for their staying together' (1972). The situationist movement, formed by Guy Debord among others, and its celebration of the experience of authenticity during ephemeral moments of liberation from capitalism were part of the same trend (Langman 2014, 193–94).[4] Following – albeit, it seems, not consciously – in the footsteps of its forerunners, the Occupy movement did not aim to transcend the here and now of the encampment: It had little sense of ideological continuities, paid scant attention to its own future and did not seem to be particularly concerned with its prospects of changing the outside world.

In the case of Occupy, but also earlier European mobilizations, such as the *Indignados*, it was the movement itself that was turned into the object of political action, while the ostensible nonexistence of ideology meant that the experience of activism became the value to guide the action. The choice was hailed by many as fulfilling the potential offered by prefigurative politics – 'the refusal to adopt formal leadership or any pre-defined ideological goal was a conscious strategy which pointed towards the kinds of possible future(s) desired' (Howard and Pratt-Boyden 2013, 729) – and as allowing Occupy to remain untainted by the corrupting mechanisms of power. Spontaneity, autonomy and related qualities assumed to inhere in the activist experience constituted the axis around which Occupy and other prefigurative mobilizations have revolved and from which this 'directionless'

(Howard and Pratt-Boyden 2013, 729) political activity obtained its (non) orientation.

As should be clear from the many discursive examples used in this chapter, the dismissal of ideology was, at least implicitly, part of the celebration of prefigurative politics. In fact, instances of explicit rejections of ideology are not in short supply either. Accordingly, prefigurative mobilizations resist 'the urge to formulate policy demands, to endorse party politics, or to embrace the worn-out ideologies of the cold war' (Harcourt 2012, 54); they 'aim to be free of ideological or institutional constraint' (Howard and Pratt-Boyden 2013, 733); they refuse 'singular demands, ideologies, or programmes for social change' (Maeckelbergh 2012, 211); they 'do not adhere to dogma and hierarchy' and are instead 'based in trust and love' (Sitrin 2006, 2). With the movement's attention focused on itself, and activism revolving around maintaining the occupation, ideology turned out to be a distraction: 'Why worry about analyses and political work if prefiguration promises a new beginning, the success of which seemingly depends only on the goodwill and the creativity of the occupants?' (Rohgalf 2013, 163). Or it could have been the other way round in that fixation with the dynamics of prefiguration may have stemmed from aversion to an ideological debate: 'A focus on group processes can reflect the avoidance of a larger discussion of goals and strategies' (Smith and Glidden 2012, 290). In any case, as Blair Taylor (2013, 739) writes, the occupation itself allowed to 'neatly fill this ideological vacuum and suspend the need for further discussion'. As a result of this evacuation of political content, the movement's 'general assemblies often had the character of rather long house meetings punctuated with political slogans':

> Listening to the general assemblies held in Zuccotti Park, one hears little discussion of political vision, policy measures, the feasibility of socialism in one country or even the Tobin Tax. Instead, most discussion centers on the logistics of maintaining the occupation: feeding people, noise issues . . . keeping warm and sleeping arrangements. (Taylor 2013, 739)

To recapitulate this analysis of Occupy, the rationale of the mobilization was to prefigure the world that the activists desired, one based on principles of horizontality and autonomy and allowing a free expression of spontaneity. The activists viewed themselves as representing everybody adversely affected by neoliberalism, the 99 percent. Due to the infinite diversity of such a constituency as well as the prefigurative nature of Occupy and its denial of ideology, the movement was unwilling to formulate a programme or a goal, even in the broadest sense of the word. It declared its members to be its demands (whatever that catchy phrase was supposed to mean) and, accordingly, turned its attention inwards, to processes and practices of activism itself. Consequently, the movement became completely self-sufficient and with no existence outside the camp – a 'temporary autonomous zone', to adapt Hakim Bey's terms – for 'you cannot occupy at a distance from an occupation' (Harcourt 2012, 45). With the passage of time, the legacy of Occupy has become a subject of a major controversy in progressive circles, a topic probably even more contentious than preceding incarnations of anti-neoliberal activism. The praise that Occupy has received, especially from commentators writing in anarchist and autonomist vein, is understandable in the context that I have already noted, namely one of disillusionment with mainstream politics, formal institutions, the state and modernity overall with its structured protocols and bureaucratic priorities.[5] But, as others have noted, 'successful protest movements aren't about camping out, book sharing, eating, and "talking to each other"' (Ostroy 2012). In the absence of an explicit ideological debate, prefigurative rituals serve to evade difficult questions of goal and strategy and blunt the edge of radical politics. The conditions of the struggle and its purpose have been obscured due to prefigurative aversion to theory and, in particular, political economy, and the enemy has been abstracted into 'them' or the '1 percent'. The last point is explored in depth in chapter 5 which engages with the 99 percent discourse to reflect upon the prospects for progressive populism and its chances to challenge neoliberal hegemony.

NOTES

1. This claim is not just intuitively correct. It is also confirmed by psychological research. Accordingly, participants of the Occupy movement (described, following American fashion, as 'liberals') tend to attach a lot of significance to their individual uniqueness, in opposition to 'conservatives' associated with the Tea Party Movement: 'liberals underestimate their similarity to other liberals . . . whereas moderates and conservatives overestimate their similarity to other moderates and conservatives' (Stern, West and Schmitt 2014, 137). This difference in participants' self-perceptions may partly explain some of the organizational tensions within and eventual fiasco of the Occupy movement and a much greater cohesion and effectiveness of 'conservative' populism.

2. Another fundamental risk of consensus is that it may, in Morgan Gibson's words (2013, 344), 'produce conformity and groupthink rather than promoting the creative and valuable role of dissent in fostering new ideas and improving old ones through conflict, debate and struggle'.

3. An exception in this respect is the discussion by a scholar and activist, Rodrigo Nunes. Nunes (2005, 311) writes: 'By becoming this transcendent ideal, horizontality

and openness – themselves not unfamiliar to business and management discourses – can become very similar to liberalism'.

4. Claims to their radical inventiveness notwithstanding, specific practices of the Occupy movement are not new either. For example, the human microphone was employed to facilitate consensus within movements in the 1980s and 1990s (Jones 2014, 154).

5. Another reason sometimes given for the elation is that the protests took place at all, after a long delay post the financial collapse and amid what seemed like a complete lethargy of society subjected for too long to paralyzing operations of neoliberal hegemony.

Chapter 5

We Are the 99 Percent . . .
But What Do We Want?

Whereas networking and prefiguration pertain to anti-neoliberal movements' preferred mode of operation, the 'We are the 99 percent' catchphrase aims to capture their political imagination – the essence of their protest against the financial crisis and related austerity policies imposed by neoliberal governments and international financial institutions. This chapter examines the populist character of the 99 percent discourse and evaluates its political limitations as well as mobilizing potential. The discussion begins with a short account of the rise of the 99 percent narrative in Occupy, its prototypes in earlier movements and some of the controversies that it has sparked. The analysis then centres on the concept of populism, the degree of its commensurability with progressive political objectives and its relationship to ideology. The chapter's argument is that populism is a 'thin' and largely indeterminate ideological category, and is as such unable, by itself, to fulfil the functions of ideology. Populism cannot provide a map for political action without first obtaining a specific articulation within more comprehensive ideological structures. Thus, as I will argue with regard to the 99 percent slogan, while it has a broad populist appeal that can bring people together – an asset that is in deficit following decades of neoliberal (de)socialization – it is insufficient, on its own, to help anti-neoliberal movements to take the next step, namely posit a political alternative to the neoliberal status quo and propose the means to pursue it.

THE STORY OF THE 99 PERCENT

We are the 99 percent. We are getting kicked out of our homes. We are forced to choose between groceries and rent. We are denied quality

medical care. We are suffering from environmental pollution. We are
working long hours for little pay and no rights, if we're working at all. We
are getting nothing while the other 1 percent is getting everything. We are
the 99 percent. ('We are the 99 percent' website: http://wearethe99percent
.tumblr.com/Introduction)

'We are the 99 percent' was the rallying cry of Occupy and has remained
part of the public lexicon following the forced clearance of the movement's
encampments all over the world. It has been hailed as an idea that authorities
could not 'evict' and hence a symbolic link between occupations in Zuccotti
Park and elsewhere and prospective successive expressions of anti-neoliberal
resistance. But while the concept has become inexorably associated with the
Occupy movement, it is – like many other anti-neoliberal themes and ideas
that are widely but wrongly assumed to be unique – neither new nor original.
As is often the case with discursive tools of anti-neoliberal activism, even a
quick investigation reveals that the concept has a much longer history than its
contemporary enthusiasts imagine. Thus, for example, the 99 percent slogan
was used by George Orwell in his wartime diary (Brass 2014, 254), whereas
its flipside, the 1 percent, featured in the Port Huron Statement, the founding
declaration of Students for a Democratic Society which 'may have been the
most widely distributed document of the American left in the sixties' (Kir-
patrick Sale in Hayden 2012). The statement, as Tom Hayden (2012) writes,
was 'prophetic in condemning the 1 percent, who in 1962 owned more than
80 percent of all personal shares of stock'. Another well-known reference to
the 99 versus 1 percent is in Howard Zinn's *A People's History of the United
States*, first published in 1980.[1]

A more immediate inspiration for Occupy's articulation of the 99 percent
leitmotif came in the form of a *Vanity Fair* article by an economist and Nobel
Prize recipient, Joseph Stiglitz (2011). The article, titled 'Of the 1%, by the
1%, for the 1%', emphasized the reality of extreme inequality in the United
States, a range of its causes and its damaging implications, especially in the
political sphere where private and corporate interests exert enormous influence further exacerbating the yawning gap between the top and the rest of
American society. David Graeber (2013, 40–41) maintained that Stiglitz's
article about the 1 percent prompted him to coin the 99 percent motto for
Occupy – a claim that was subsequently ridiculed by Tom Brass (2014, 254)
as exposing Graeber's eagerness to partake in neoliberal academia's 'competitive rush to assert property rights over long-established ideas'. In any
case, once associated with Occupy, the idea quickly expanded within and
beyond the movement. To popularize the moniker, a Tumblr website was
set up (http://wearethe99percent.tumblr.com) where members of the 99 percent, but also some 1-percenters who sympathized with the narrative, could

post their photographs with accompanying stories of personal hardship and discontent. The introduction to the website addresses its visitors and contributors as ordinary, hard-working Americans who nevertheless suffer from acute economic insecurity:

> You're someone who doesn't know whether there's going to be enough money to make this month's rent. You're someone who gets sick and toughs it out because you'll never afford the hospital bills. You're someone who's trying to move a mountain of debt that never seems to get any smaller no matter how hard you try. You do all the things you're supposed to do. You buy store brands. You get a second job. You take classes to improve your skills. But it's not enough. It's never enough. The anxiety, the frustration, the powerlessness is still there, hovering like a storm crow. Every month you make it is a victory, but a Pyrrhic one – once you're over the hump, all you can do is think about the next one and how much harder it's all going to be. ('We are the 99 percent' website: http://wearethe99percent.tumblr.com/Introduction)

As is evident in this quote, the discourse of the 99 percent is devoid of explicitly politically charged words or an overt ideological identification – a characteristic I have already stressed in other discursive expressions of anti-neoliberal contestation. The emphasis is on the precariousness and a sense of economic vulnerability experienced by individuals in spite of them making every reasonable effort to avoid destitution. In other words, the narrative revolves around the breakdown of the American Dream. In the wake of the financial crisis this explains its ability to attract the increasingly squeezed middle classes and to capitalize on the widespread outrage with the tiny minority of people who bear the responsibility for the turmoil but who have consolidated their extraordinary privileges in its aftermath. Indeed, the slogan appeared to resonate so well with life experiences of large sections of the American populace that it was promptly seized by politicians, businesses and the media:

> Soon there were income calculators ('What Percent Are You?' asked The Wall Street Journal), music playlists (an album of Woody Guthrie covers, promoted as a 'soundtrack for the 99 percent') and cheap lawn signs. And, inevitably, there were ads: a storefront near Union Square peddles 'Gifts for the 99 percent'. A trailer for a Showtime television series about management consultants, 'House of Lies', describes the lead characters as 'the 1 percent sticking it to the 1 percent'. A Craigslist ad for a three-bedroom apartment in Brooklyn has the come-on 'Live Like the 1 Percent!' (Stelter 2011)

While media-friendly, and supposedly putting the 1 percent on the defensive in the national and global conversation, the 99 versus 1 percent dichotomy has not been left unchallenged. For example, in the United States, conservative opponents of Occupy, under the aegis of a blogger and radio host, Eric Erickson, set up their own website – '53 percent' – claiming that the number matched the percentage of Americans who at that time paid income taxes and contrasting them with the 47 percent supposedly dependent on the government (http://the53.tumblr.com). The website is similar in style to the 99 percent Tumblr; it features pictures and stories of American citizens, either well-to-do people boasting about their wealth and how they earned it solely by a lifetime of hard work or poor folks who are nevertheless too proud to 'scrounge' from the state and who never waver in their belief that thrift, frugality and hard work will bring them a better future. Puritan ethics permeates these personal stories as well as underpinning their authors' contempt both for state dependants in the '47 percent' and for the exponents of the 99 percent narrative. The latter are portrayed either as spoiled, privileged middle-class kids or as a lazy and demoralized 'underclass', and always as individuals with an undue sense of entitlement. Admittedly, the '53 versus 47 percent' counter-narrative has never managed to gain popularity on a par with the 99 percent meme. What is more, his attack on the 47 percent turned out to be one of the blunders of Mitt Romney's unsuccessful 2012 presidential campaign.

Still, the concept of the 99 percent has also stirred some controversies among sympathetic commentators, and these are symptomatic of its broader problems that I will discuss shortly. One issue relates to the fact that 99 percent is an extremely wide-ranging group, 'a mix of the wretched of the earth and a (fairly thick) stratum of the upper middle class: doctors, university teachers, journalists, senior management, PR and senior civil servants' (Halimi 2017). In fact, the income threshold qualifying for membership in the top 1 percent in the United States was US$389,000 in 2011, the year of Occupy (Sahadi 2014). On the one hand, it is hard to imagine that large numbers of people on salaries just below that sum would identify with the 99 percent narrative. This is compounded by the fact that many Americans believe themselves to be far wealthier, in relation to the rest of US society, than they are in reality; for example, in 2003 '19% of US taxpayers thought they already belonged to the top 1% by income; a further 20% thought they would soon be part of it' (Halimi 2017). On the other hand, even individuals on six-figure salaries do not share the lifestyles of the very top where the concentration of wealth is at its most extreme. Hence, economist Paul Krugman suggested that 'the 99 percent slogan aims too low. A large fraction of the top 1 percent's gains have actually gone to an even smaller group, the top 0.1 percent – the richest one-thousandth of the population' (Krugman 2011).

It has been argued that the mobilizing power of the 99 percent discourse trumps any issues with the income threshold it uses to highlight the economic divide in society: 'the naming of the antagonism has some attachment to empirical facts, but need not be bound by them' (Srnicek and Williams 2015, 160). This is a valid point, but the underlying assumption of an all-inclusive nature of the narrative has nevertheless had some problematic implications. The idea that the movement was in principle able to bring together (almost) everyone in society – from the top of the middle class to homeless people – as one group somehow capable of political agency is a counter-productive fiction. The narrative has also been undermined by exclusions that were blatant in Occupy's practices and narratives. For example, as I noted in chapter 4, questions have been raised concerning the extent to which the ability to participate and feel welcome in the movement depended on class, gender or ethnicity. The claim to inclusiveness is further contradicted by the movement's failure to pay adequate attention to immigrants and the hardships that they face (Taylor 2017, 178–79). Another thorny question pertains to political or class loyalties of some groups or professions that were discursively included as members of the exploited majority. Thus, one dispute within Occupy Wall Street (OWS) revolved around whether the police are the 99 percent. As Jeremy Kessler (2011) reported, many signs in Zuccotti Park expressed solidarity with the police: '"The Working Class Must Unite (Hey, Cops, That Includes You)", "Dear NYPD – join us. You are also the 99 percent" – and occupiers frequently [broke] ranks to joke with officers late into the evening'. Others within as well as outside Occupy have been very critical of such an 'ecumenical' stance: 'It's essential to understand that, regardless of their class origins, the police are the army of capital historically born out of southern slave patrols and industrial labor disputes' (Bray 2013, 158).

Taken in isolation, the significance of each of the previously mentioned dilemmas is not such that they could undercut the activist mobilization or seriously compromise the narrative underpinning it. However, they are all linked to a broader issue, namely the amorphous and indeterminate nature of this discourse. While a great phrase to highlight the outrageous concentration of wealth, power and privilege in a tiny minority, the 99 versus 1 percent 'conceals as much as it reveals' (Taylor 2013, 742). Like the population that it claims to represent, the 99 percent is an extremely capacious concept, and the rhetoric of it is indefinitely vague and woolly, as in 'it is easy to see what the movement is demanding: quite simply, a world that works for the 99%' (Van Gelder 2011, 6). It is my contention that Occupy's dependence on this thin and nebulous ideational foundation was one of the movement's main discursive limitations. Averse to theoretical analysis and openly ideological debate, Occupy did not fill the mould of the 99 percent with political content 'thick' enough to articulate its aims and means. It thus did not move beyond representing just an outburst of frustration and anger – loud and desperate, but ultimately undisruptive to the neoliberal system.

The rest of this chapter engages with the rhetoric of Occupy, as well as parallel claims advanced in related anti-neoliberal mobilizations, as an instance of populist discourse. Populism is a discursive style which contrasts the 'people', whom it means to represent, with a parasitic and exploitative minority, as in the 99 versus 1 percent. It is typically conceptualized as a 'thin' ideology (Mudde 2007; Stanley 2008) in that, aside from drawing the sharp distinction between the people and the elite, 'it does little else' (Freeden 2003, 98). In view of that, and anticipating the argument that follows, populism *in itself* is too narrow to be able to determine what is so virtuous about the majority that it claims to embody and, accordingly, what are the objectives that it aims to pursue on its behalf. Anything that populism 'does' in its concrete articulations (by individuals, parties or movements) beyond drawing that basic contrast can only stem from an ideological identity that it acquires by becoming associated with a broader ideological system. However, in the case of Occupy and similar protests, that association has been only tentative and implicit owing to their rejection of overt ideological commitments. As a result, the 99 versus 1 percent has remained just an inchoate expression of the populist antagonism with no translation into a political programme or set of demands. The next section elaborates upon this point by combining some theoretical insights into the nature of populism with discursive examples drawn from recent anti-neoliberal movements.[2]

ANTI-NEOLIBERAL POPULISM: WHAT IS MISSING?

Occupy Wall Street is a leaderless resistance movement with people of many colors, genders and political persuasions. The one thing we all have in common is that We Are The 99% that will no longer tolerate the greed and corruption of the 1%. ('Occupy Wall Street' website: http://occupy wallst.org/)

Populism has attracted a lot of interest of late due to the endurance or, in some recent cases, unprecedented success of European far right parties, such as the French *Front National* or the Dutch *Partij voor de Vrijheid* ('Party for Freedom'), the Brexit vote in the United Kingdom in June 2016 and, above all, the election of Donald Trump as the President of the United States in November of the same year. Populism tends to be associated mainly with such nationalistic and inward-looking reactions to globalization (Soborski 2013, 117–23) but the label applies as well to left-wing parties, for example, the Spanish *Podemos* or the Greek *Syriza* (acronym for 'Coalition of the Radical Left') (Kioupkiolis 2016; Stavrakakis and Katsambekis 2014) and broader progressive political trends, such as the Pink Tide – a shift leftwards in much of Latin American politics that began in early 2000s (Wylde 2012) and has ebbed since the centre-right regained ground in Argentina and Brazil in 2015 and 2016, respectively. Indeed, it is increasingly argued that the left should reclaim the term with pride and make every effort to counter the populism of the right with one of its own (e.g., Jones 2016). Another debate on populism concerns the role of leaders. Some scholars have argued that populism is a political stance that involves a top-down chain of command and assigns a central role to leadership, regardless of whether this is to pursue a left- or right-wing agenda (de la Torre 2016; Filc 2015). It would follow that the 'post-representative' movements covered in this book could not be classified as populist (Moffitt 2016). However, other analysts have relied solely on the already noted, more elementary characteristic – namely, 'the Manichean distinction between "the pure people" and "the corrupt elite"' (Mudde and Rovira Kaltwasser 2011, 7). Accordingly, populism 'can be left wing as well as right wing, and it can be organized in both top-down and bottom-up fashion' (Mudde and Rovira Kaltwasser 2011, 7). My argument follows the latter line of thought.

The capacity of populism to serve both right- and left-wing purposes as well as support a variety of organizational forms stems from it having a chameleon-like nature or, in a poetic turn of phrase, an 'empty heart' (Taggart 2004, 275). This is a key point about populism from the perspective of the present argument. As I have already highlighted, in contrast to full ideologies – liberalism, socialism or conservatism, each offering a distinctive and comprehensive worldview – populism is a thin ideological current, and as such unable, in itself, to articulate a vision that could act as a political map for individuals or groups. Populism is more of a style of political communication, which may become associated with a plethora of diverse ideologies on the left as well as the right, than an ideological category of its own (Taggart 2004, 275). Its particular articulations are normally attached to established ideologies and imbued with specific meanings in the light of the conceptual arrangements of their hosts. So, for instance, national populism is a combination of populist discourse with conservative nationalism as evident in political agendas laid out in manifestos of some far right parties. National populism concretizes the fundamental populist antagonism – people against elites – by imbuing it with conservative nationalist meanings. Accordingly, it is the 'real' ethnic members of the national community that need to be liberated from their mistreatment at the hands of cosmopolitan elites. The elites aim to erode the organic bonds of the nation in order to make it easier to manipulate the people. They do this by promoting globalization and, in particular, immigration – immigrants ending up as the primary targets of national populist resentment. In turn, the socialist version of populism tends to define the people in terms of their socio-economic class, sometimes also colour, and the elites as capitalists and imperialists. This is, of course, a very crude description, but the point is that it is the socialist framing that provides the conceptual foundation on which left-wing populist arguments and narratives about the majority-minority antagonism can rely. For example, the more radical currents of Pink Tide politics, in particular *Chavismo*, instill the basic populist structure with a distinctively socialist content: The resulting ideational combination is extensive enough to sustain a relatively comprehensive political vision. In a nutshell, it is the broader ideological backdrops, rather than populism's meagre core, that allow populists of different shades to articulate their particular goals and posit the measures to pursue them.

Now, the issue with the populist discourse adopted by anti-neoliberal movements discussed in this book is that it tends to remain at the level of a bare opposition between the elites and the masses and so, devoid of adequate ideological scaffolding, is unable to move beyond mere 'platitudes about equality and fairness' (Winlow et al. 2015, 155). Yet again, at the heart of the problem is ideology or rather its neglect. Oblivious to the need for an overt ideological vision, the 99 percent discourse has relied solely on basic anti-elitist instincts and remained politically amorphous. It should be noted that while the focus of this chapter has been primarily on Occupy as the clearest exemplification of the problem, its 99 percent narrative has developed alongside similar arguments in other recent anti-neoliberal movements and mobilizations. For example, the 'we are one hand' slogan of the 2011 Egyptian uprising stressed the unity of the people as transcending any religious or ethnic divisions (Gerbaudo 2012, 10). Likewise, the *Indignados* movement in Europe saw itself as representing ordinary citizens against self-serving elites. Here, Occupy's 1 percent had its equivalent in *la Casta* ('the caste') or 'Troika', a decision-making group consisting of the European Commission, the European Central Bank and the International Monetary Fund. The Troika has been in charge of the policies of extreme austerity imposed on Greece and other European countries and is a convenient symbol for everything that is wrong with the neoliberal system. Going further back in time, the slogan of the 2001 popular rebellion in Argentina, *Que se vayan todos* ('Out with them all') represented the same popular outrage with the corrupted elite clique at the top. In all these instances, a dismissive if not outrightly hostile attitude to ideology has meant that the movements were halted at what is essentially a pre-political stage: an outburst of anger and an enthused proclamation of popular unity but without any clear idea of political direction or purpose.

In light of the largely negative coverage that populism tends to receive from mainstream media, I should stress once again that it is not the populist orientation of anti-neoliberal movements that as such should be viewed as their weakness. In fact, to take again the example of Occupy, its focus on the 99 versus 1 percent theme was probably a smart strategy to use at the outset of the mobilization. As David Meyer noted at that time, 'To succeed movement campaigns identify a base and a target, framing their core constituency as worthy – and preferably numerous. The target should be identifiable too. Deciding whom to blame is a key task of all politics, including movement politics' (Meyer 2011). It should also be acknowledged that the majoritarian orientation of recent mobilizations contrasts favourably with centrifugal tendencies of earlier movements. The emphasis on the unity of the people implies a possibility of overcoming the trend towards fragmentation which is inherent in identitarian politics. In one unequivocal assessment (Winlow et al. 2015, 152), the centripetal character of recent protests 'transcended the debilitating logic of identity politics which had bogged down the Left since the 1960s'. What is more, the fact that this popular unity was conceived in opposition to the establishment signalled a possibility that the movements would engage with questions of capitalism and political economy. Indeed, Occupy's slogans 'had an appealing air of class antagonism' (Winlow et al. 2015, 152). The problem was, however, that neither Occupy nor other recent anti-neoliberal movements channelled that antagonism and anger towards a political goal. As Srnicek and Williams (2015, 161) put it,

> A vision of the future is essential to a proper populism, and it is what many recent populist movements have lacked. Occupy, for instance, never translated the negative moment of insubordination into a positive political project around which the people could be organised. It never combined diverse interests into a project for a better future, remaining at the negative level of rejection.

This criticism is reinforced by a quick reflection upon some other discursive themes that have been invoked, alongside 99 percent, to symbolize anti-neoliberal activism post the financial crash. In the case of *Indignados*, the focal point of the movement is given in the name itself – the emotion of indignation is at the heart of the protest. In a similar vein, the opening act of the Arab Spring (in Tunisia) was dubbed 'Revolution of Dignity' (Aleya-Sghaier 2012). As for Occupy, activist scholars supplemented the 99 percent discourse with emphasis on the overarching conditions of 'precarity' (Butler 2011) or 'vulnerability' (Fadaee and Schindler 2015). But while these may indeed be accurate descriptions of the feelings that prevailed among the activists, expression of feelings is not sufficient to sustain a durable movement. It may be relatively straightforward to identify the reasons for indignation – national and global levels of inequality today are obviously shockingly high – but the question of what to do with the system that generates them is not thereby addressed. Ditto for precariousness or vulnerability: realization of the collective sharing of these conditions may have a therapeutic effect on those affected by them but does not help the precariat to move beyond a mere recognition of the fact. The role of feelings and emotions in political action should not be underappreciated and yet, in themselves, without a vision and strategy, they do not take activists very far.

The pre-political populism that has prevailed in anti-neoliberal movements in recent years is related to their other characteristics discussed in this book. It resonates with the dominant activist interpretation of networking and horizontalism: One reason why the 99 percent narrative failed to name the system at the root of its grievances was that such an assertion would risk activating divisions between the diverse constituents of anti-neoliberal politics broadly conceived, and hence an inevitable contest for influence. The critique has thus been reduced to a moralistic outrage with individual greed rather than providing any analysis of the conditions that allow it to reign supreme. The vagueness of its populist orientation is also compatible with anti-neoliberal activism's emphasis on prefiguration. Occupations and their rituals conferred on the participants a sense of belonging with others equally let down by the 1 percent; the nature of that experience supposedly prefiguring the alternative to the world where '1 percent is getting everything'. Thus, although the populist move towards transcending the fragmented nature of the politics of particular identities has been a positive development within recent anti-neoliberal movements, their new approach stopped at an abstraction of a mere numerical aggregate that was not pegged to any project of transformation. Without a set of values to guide it, the 99 percent remained an imagined community without a purpose, a community that did not really know what it wanted except that it did not like how things were in society.

Connections between the motives behind anti-neoliberal movements' fixation with networking, their commitment to prefigurative politics and the undeveloped populism of the 99 percent discourse mean that their respective implications are likewise intertwined. For example, aside from its limited political efficacy, another problem stemming from the ideological thinness of recent anti-neoliberal discourses is their susceptibility to co-optation by neoliberal hegemony, a liability that I have discussed in relation to other facets of contemporary anti-neoliberalism.[3] It has also been argued that movements like Occupy, which conferred on activists a sense of inclusiveness and shared vulnerability, have in effect served as a safety valve to release their anger and frustration. They have therefore been functional from the point of view of the neoliberal system; they have allowed its continuing expansion while providing its discontents with an opportunity for a collective healing:

> It is imperative, when faced with such protests, to ask: what has changed as a result? . . . If the remaining logic is simply that the protest enables pissed-off individuals to cathartically release their pent-up frustration and momentarily draw strength from being around others who feel the same way, before returning to their lives to again be subject to the same objective causes of their frustration, then we can begin to see the limitations that have been imposed upon democratic political protest. (Winlow et al. 2015, 164; see also Taylor 2017, 242)

The hazy nature of recent forms of anti-neoliberal populism may also render it susceptible to absorption by the extreme right: 'A vague constellation of populist themes and anti-banker sentiment coupled with scepticism towards the traditional left, theory and politics as such could just as easily be channelled in non-emancipatory responses to economic inequality' (Taylor 2013, 743). As I have emphasized, the ideational thinness of populism means that it needs to rest on values and ideals to inform the basic antagonism at its centre. As long as such a foundation is missing, populist rhetoric is politically meaningless – until the point, that is, when it finds its voice. The trouble is that the right seems ready to give it that opportunity and hence harness the rising tide of populist sentiments to its own agenda.

OWS has become a memorable meme, and mainstream media have helped, for better or for worse, to shape its identity. In one such intervention, one symptomatic of the issues that I have discussed, a CNN correspondent and *New York Times* reporter, Brian Stelter (2011) affirmed:

> Whatever the long-term effects of the Occupy movement, protesters have succeeded in implanting 'We are the 99 percent' . . . into the cultural and political lexicon. . . . Easily grasped in its simplicity and Twitter-friendly in its brevity, the slogan has practically dared listeners to pick a side.

The first part of this assessment seems accurate, but as for the second part the question arises whether this is a meaningful or consequential choice? Thus far, what anti-neoliberal populism has been able to put forward is a discursive alternative between the well-being of humanity and a further consolidation of the global plutocracy. Phrased in this way, the choice is obviously a 'no-brainer', but politics reduced to declaring sides in a struggle defined in such sweeping terms does not stand for much. Talk is cheap, as the saying goes, particularly when it does not involve any strategy, programme or vision aside from 'humanity minus the oligarchs' (Halimi 2017).

In conclusion, the 99 versus 1 percent narrative has arrested the development of progressive resistance against the system that had caused unprecedented inequalities and climaxed with the calamity of the recent financial crisis. As Craig Calhoun (2013, 34) notes, 'The brilliant slogan about the "99%" and the "1%" almost swallowed the movement. It was hard for any more particular issue to compete with it'. Some have considered the 'non-ideological veneer' of the 99 percent terminology an advantage, at least in the United States, in the context of 'the American liberal fetishization of "non-ideological" popular discontent' (Bray 2013: 158, 301). However, although a 'seemingly nonideological space' (Bray 2013, 157) associated with the discourse may have helped mobilize a broad support quickly, it has condemned the movement to what is basically a pre-political stage of protest without a plan or purpose. The activist emphasis on the 99 percent went hand in hand with celebration of the fact that 'every possible demand, critique and proposal was present in the movement' and that 'the movements demanded everything and nothing at the same time' (Castells 2015, 125, 188). Descriptions of this kind – and it is worth noting that the ones just cited were put forward with approval by an enthusiastic supporter – may help explain why Occupy was more a 'moment' than a 'movement' (Calhoun 2013). The next and final chapter considers, in a broad and open-ended way, how taking ideology seriously could be a step towards a more effective, lasting and meaningful change.

NOTES

1. Zinn (2015, 632) wrote: 'One percent of the nation owns a third of the wealth. The rest of the wealth is distributed in such a way as to turn those in the 99 percent against one another: small property owners against the propertyless, black against white, native-born against foreign-born, intellectuals and professionals against the uneducated and unskilled. These groups have resented one another and warred against one another with such vehemence and violence as to obscure their common position as sharers of leftovers in a very wealthy country. Against the reality of that desperate, bitter battle for resources made scarce by elite control, I am taking the liberty of uniting those 99 percent as "the people". I have been writing a history that attempts to represent their submerged, deflected, common interest'.

2. However, this is not a place to embark on a lengthy review of the rich scholarship on populism as an ideological category. Readers interested in the topic may start by consulting the chapter by Cas Mudde and Cristóbal Rovira Kaltwasser in *The Oxford Handbook of Political Ideologies* (2013).

3. Elective affinities between neoliberalism and populism have been highlighted by others in relation to broader left-wing populism as well (Johnson 2017, 87).

Chapter 6

Ideology for the Future of Progressive Activism

At its outset, the 2007–2008 financial crisis cast a serious doubt over neoliberalism's capacity to survive and led to a revival of hopes for a profound restructuring of the capitalist system. A rare opportunity for the political left seemed within reach, and anti-neoliberal movements were at the centre of everybody's attention. Ten years later, the state of affairs could not be further from those expectations, and questions are being asked as to the reasons for the ongoing erosion of progressive politics and concomitant reconsolidation of neoliberalism. Ideology is slowly gaining recognition as an important element in political activism; the neglect of it by anti-neoliberal movements is noted more often than before, though still rarely systematically examined, as a reason for their disappointing record. Some theorists have also proposed various criteria for an ideological vision that, they believe, could challenge the hegemony of neoliberalism. This chapter refrains from making any prescriptive claims concerning the specific content of a counter-hegemonic ideology but highlights a number of broad characteristics that would strengthen its relevance and appeal in anticipation of the next political opening.

UPS AND DOWNS OF ANTI-NEOLIBERAL ACTIVISM

It is a fact of the information age that too many movements spring up like beautiful flowers but quickly die off. It's because they don't have roots. And they don't have long-term plans for how they are going to sustain themselves. So when storms come, they get washed away. (Klein 2011, 46)

Naomi Klein's words quoted here were uttered to the occupiers of the Zuccotti Park on 6 October 2011, less than six weeks before the NYPD began
clearing the park. Echoing many on the left, Klein expressed her belief that
Occupy Wall Street would last, unlike the global justice movement of the
preceding decade. By the time of Occupy it was reluctantly acknowledged by
many sympathetic and insider commentators, like Klein herself, that the preceding global justice movement had failed to sustain its momentum into the
first decade of the twenty-first century. Consequently, faced with little effective resistance, neoliberalism kept on its steady expansion until it ultimately
plunged the world into financial chaos. In 2011, it was thus Occupy's turn to
become the beacon of progressive hope: 'This time', continued Klein (2011,
48), 'our movement cannot get distracted, divided, burned out, or swept away
by events. This time we have to succeed'.

    In 2011 many progressives were, like Klein, understandably excited about
the delayed yet captivating wave of protests against the neoliberal response
to the consequences of the crisis and neoliberal system overall. For example,
Immanuel Wallerstein (2011) cheered the Occupy movement as a great success in spite of the challenges that it was likely to face: 'Rome wasn't built
in a day', he said, quite reasonably. Others concurred: 'Whatever happens
next, Occupy Wall Street has already accomplished something that changes
everything. It has fundamentally altered the national conversation' (Van
Gelder 2011, 11). The debate about Occupy has been ongoing since the end
of the encampments with contributors trying to take stock of the movement's
legacy. Many of the evaluations relate to activist principles discussed in this
book, such as prefiguration. Castells, for example, acknowledged a lack of
tangible consequences of the 99 percent movement but asserted that prefigurative politics meant that 'true transformation was taking place in people's
minds' (Castells 2015, 145). This was allegedly confirmed by sociological
surveys, but the specific outcomes that he invoked are not awe-inspiring:
a political campaign on Facebook had drawn 54,900 'likes' (195), and a
certain 'uneasiness became pervasive among the most active components of
the movement' (144).[1] Other accounts highlighted Occupy's ability to adapt
to new challenges and emphasized the effectiveness of Occupy Sandy in
responding to the hurricane (Welty 2014, 45). Still others affirmed its contribution to Barack Obama's re-election (Langman 2013, 522). The latter point
contrasts sharply with the bitter disappointment that Obama's presidency
engendered amongst some (other) left-wingers. That disillusionment, of
course, is put into perspective in comparison with more recent developments
in the United States, namely the rise of far right populism whose culmina-
tion, so far, has been Donald Trump's election as Obama's successor and the
ongoing implications of it. Elsewhere, ten years after the credit crunch, and
six following Occupy, the situation does not look any more appealing from

a progressive point of view. Britain's political reality is now one of Brexit peppered with rising xenophobia, extreme austerity and squeeze on wages. Central Europe is embracing conservative populism. In Latin America the Pink Tide is being reversed. In China and Russia autocracy is in full swing, while a return to it is taking place in Turkey and the Philippines among other places. The list could go on and on.

While the developments mentioned here are of miscellaneous nature and cannot all be related directly to failures of movements like Occupy, they nevertheless pose a serious question mark over the broad impact of anti-neoliberal activism. The latter is hard to measure, of course, as effects of social movements can be 'diffuse, indirect, subtle, and long-term' (Ganesh and Stohl 2013, 447). However, although it is also right to say that 'we need to credit the simple survival of activists and ideas' (Toynbee 2009, 116), it would take a Pollyanna-like perspective on the world to claim that movements against neoliberalism have succeeded in using its crisis to their advantage. More common nowadays is thus a sense of frustration and impatience. Questions like, 'Is there a point at which a critical mass of consciousness-raising will be ready for action?' (Srnicek and Williams 2015, 7) are increasingly asked, and a range of self-reflexive critiques have been deployed on the left to account for the disappointing outcomes of latest mobilizations.

Critiques of anti-neoliberal politics revolve in particular around issues of strategy and the movements' relationship to existing political structures and institutions.[2] Questions of ideology are not usually viewed as of key importance in such accounts, but there are a few exceptions. It should be noted that while interest in the role of ideology in political activism has increased following the decline of recent anti-neoliberal protests, a concern with the left's neglect of the ideological domain was raised already in the 1980s. For example, Stuart Hall wrote in 1988 that 'in the struggle for ideas, the battle for hearts and minds . . . bad ideas can only be replaced by better, more appropriate ones' (Hall 1988, 73). Speaking of Thatcherism and resistance to it, Hall further argued that good ideas 'don't fall off the shelf without an ideological framework to give those ideas coherence . . . a perspective on what is happening to society now, a vision of the future, a capacity to articulate these vividly through a few clearly-enunciated theses or principles' (Hall 1988, 271). At roughly the same time, Colin Leys (1990, 128) spoke of the 'question of hegemony' and 'the enormity of the long-run ideological task: the construction of a new "social imaginary" '. Among more current contributions, Alain Badiou (2012, 42) emphasized 'the urgency of a reformulated ideological proposal, a powerful Idea, a pivotal hypothesis', Jonathan Pugh (2011, 295) highlighted the need for 'grand narrative' and 'the details of the Ideal city' and Simon Winlow et al. (2015, 156) argued that for political change to happen, 'basic ideological precepts capable of transforming the way the individual understands his relationship to the socio-economic system need to be in place'. Still, appreciation of ideology continues to be an exception rather than a rule in the literature that is close or internal to anti-neoliberal movements. Indeed, a defined political vision tends to be viewed as, at best, an irrelevance and, at worst, an impairment to be overcome through activist practice.

In the course of this book I have repeatedly challenged the negative view of ideology in discourses of anti-neoliberal activism. My contention is that what activists need, perhaps above all else, is a compelling ideological narrative. To be sure, activist mobilization will, inevitably and regardless of declarations to the contrary, be guided by a set of ideological beliefs. But while anti-neoliberal movements are, like all others, inescapably ideology-laden, by denying their ideological identity they cut themselves off from the resources obtainable from established traditions of political thought. Furthermore, the argument that I have developed is that the very supposition of visionless activism has been politically counter-productive. On the one hand, it may be linked to the extent within anti-neoliberal politics of what one veteran activist (who happened to take ideas seriously) derided as 'lifestyle anarchism', a faddish, easily co-opted and commodifiable form of tokenistic political engagement (Bookchin 1995).[3] On the other hand, the neglect of ideology may have given undue credence to the neoliberal pronouncement of irrelevance of alternative socio-political projects. At the climax of its hegemony in the 1990s, neoliberalism declared ideology to be dead (neoliberalism itself is not an ideology, it has been asserted, but merely an optimal, entirely pragmatic response to the natural forces of the market). In this context, it may seem paradoxical that the assumption that ideology has now become irrelevant has been so enthusiastically endorsed by many activists who otherwise oppose neoliberal theory and practice.

One explanation of this hostility towards ideology has been hinted at earlier in this book. The very system that the anti-neoliberal movements are challenging defines not just the structures within which they operate but also the conceptual material that is available to them, and so, to some extent, also the way they think. Thus, the post-ideological climate, while cohering with the dominant interests, has also permeated oppositional discourses. Furthermore, the alleged erosion of ideology, touted by neoliberals, has been reinforced by some influential social theorists who related it to a number of postmodern dynamics: scepticism towards modernity's belief in social progress, priority of cultural and religious distinctions over class identification, deterritorialization and its consequences for nationalism, the effects of the mass media on political protocols and priorities and so on (for a short overview, see Soborski 2013, 1–8). While some such assertions of a new paradigm may be valid to some extent, Justin Rosenberg's criticism of the inflated claims by scholars and commentators announcing the arrival of an all-change era is not unsubstantiated: 'Instead of deconstructing the popular *Zeitgeist*, they elevated it to the role of an intellectual *Weltgeist*' (2005, 7). What can be said at the very least is that social science has on the whole been more inclined to identify rupture than to appreciate continuity with the past in recent developments. Finally, in addition to the hegemonic impact of neoliberalism and uncurbed imagination prevailing in some segments of social science, parts of the legacy of the traditional left have also contributed to the aversion to explicit ideological work among anti-neoliberal movements. Indeed, the cul-de-sacs of the old left, especially its rigid hierarchies and commitment to industrialism without limits, and its neglect of a range of identity-related questions, are regularly invoked in arguments rejecting ideology in favour of horizontal and prefigurative activism.

While the end of ideology assertion is a hegemonic construct serving to facilitate a further depoliticization of society, the trends and factors mentioned earlier should not be dismissed altogether when considering the nature of ideological dilemmas facing the politics of anti-neoliberal resistance. Hyperbolic claims of some social theorists notwithstanding, societies today are certainly more complex, more diverse and increasingly ridden by divisions that were not fully recognized in the modern era when social struggles were defined in more monolithic terms, delimited territorially and led by national parties and trade unions. Anti-neoliberal movements' structures and strategies aim, more or less successfully, to reflect the multifaceted nature of the contemporary society, and any effective progressive ideological project would likewise need to take this diversity into account. But such an ideology would also have to reconcile acceptance of pluralism with a unifying vision, firm argument and tangible policy targets. This book is not intended as a manifesto or normative argument setting an agenda for the politics of anti-neoliberalism. What is proposed in the following section is merely a short sketch of broad criteria for an ideological narrative with a counter-hegemonic potential.

TOWARDS COUNTER-HEGEMONY

We are the ones, we militants without a strategy of emancipation, who are (and who have been for some time now) the real aphasics! (Badiou 2013, 45)

The movements discussed in this book view themselves as radical in their eschewal of conventional political engagement and preference for an alternative repertoire of action. However, the etymology of the word *radical(ism)* has to do with roots (*radix* in Latin). It follows that a radical movement is one that goes to the origin of the problem(s) that it wants to address or challenge. If so, then in keeping with my argument in this book, anti-neoliberal movements have yet to prove their radical credentials. Thus far, the abstraction of the '1 percent' and the associated moralistic condemnation of individual greed that has been ubiquitous in discourses of anti-neoliberalism precluded any systematic analysis of the nature and *roots* of neoliberal hegemony. Meanwhile, their fixation with networking and prefiguration has focused the movements' attention on the experience of activism itself rather than on a meaningful discussion of alternatives to the state of affairs outside the spaces of encampment, protest or riot. In all fairness, this avoidance of difficult questions is partly explained by the overwhelming complexity of dilemmas that any serious attempt to destabilize the neoliberal status quo would have to face. But the fact that the world is enormously complex does not make this evasion any less futile and counter-productive.

   Still, the depth of problems potentially confronting the movements, the array of hard choices to be made and the weight of compromises to be considered are all bewildering. Thus, for example, one fundamental question is whether the blame for what is wrong with the world is to be laid on the capitalist system as such, the neoliberal incarnation of it, its globalization, the state or a combination of some of those and other factors. If blame rests on capitalism per se, then myriad questions arise again. Should a revolutionary path be taken in order to defeat the capital and, if so, what exactly would revolution in the twenty-first century entail? What would constitute the first step? Should the state be destroyed or reclaimed for a non-capitalist future? Who would lead the revolution, or would there be no leaders? And so on, and so forth. Alternatively, it can be specifically the harsh and wild neoliberal incarnation of capitalism that is blamed for having led the world to the precipice on which it now stands. In such a case, should a neo-Keynesian, social-democratic model be pursued instead of the so-called free-market capitalism? If so, is it to be enacted on a global level to permit an extension to everyone on the planet of the rights and responsibilities once conferred solely within the confines of the nation state? If that is the case, then how is nationalism to be overcome, and a genuinely cosmopolitan perspective achieved, so that a Brit, or an American, accepts to bear the burden of taxation intended for raising the standard of living in, for instance, Bangladesh? If, on the other hand, social democracy is to be organized on merely national scales, as some globalization sceptics recommend, how are questions of international competition to be addressed, particularly in the face of transnational challenges such as climate change? Is national protectionism an answer to any of the predicaments? Or, on the contrary, should any type of nationalism be uncovered (again) as the 'opium' distracting the masses' attention from the real origin of their misfortunes? Concomitantly, should the state be exposed as always an ally of the capital, in which case the Keynesian phase would have been an exception confirming the rule: possible only in its specific spatial and temporal context and ultimately functional for the system by preventing a more meaningful challenge to it from materializing? What is the alternative then: communitarian localization and decentralization perhaps? But that would generate yet another set of thorny questions. It goes without saying that all of these dilemmas are easier articulated than tackled.

The political world today is undoubtedly extremely difficult to grasp, and none of the choices highlighted before, and selected from a much broader range of possibilities, provides the ultimate answer to the challenges that we face. Indeed, any universally accepted response would mean a closure of the discussion, and thus an end of ideology, something that will remain impossible as long as society as we know and can imagine it, exists. The problem is, though, that the extraordinary complexity of contemporary politics has led some thinkers to give up altogether on debating systemic alternatives to the current neoliberal configuration. As I noted earlier, the postmodern evasion of several fundamental political questions has influenced arguments, narratives and tactics of many anti-neoliberal movements. Faced with the perplexing variety of implications of different political options as well as philosophical and ideological considerations involved in choosing one target or solution over another, the majority of participants of anti-neoliberal movements decided to find refuge in the here and now of activism. They have resigned themselves to a stance that dismisses politics and ideology as irrelevant. It is as though engaging activists in an overt discussion of difficult political questions would spoil the fun of their being together. From the angle of prefigurative politics, as it has been understood in recent instances of activism, setting objectives and issuing demands is viewed as something to be avoided in case this leads to divisions and hence destabilizes the consensual climate of activism. Meanwhile, ideological struggles are of course ongoing in the background, unacknowledged as such, and those disagreeing with the prevailing ethos of avoiding disagreements are 'excommunicated' by reluctant intellectual gurus of supposedly leaderless movements.

Evading explicit ideological work does not mean that ideas cease to make the world go round – it only means the ideas of others prevail. It follows that anti-neoliberal movements would benefit from taking ideology seriously and engaging in the battle of ideas. While a normative argument is not something I want to pursue here, I conjecture that there are some requirements that anti-neoliberal movements would probably benefit from addressing when they set out to articulate their political stances. I will limit my discussion to one such criterion, admittedly a very broad one: 'unity in diversity'. It may be a clichéd slogan but it seems to capture the nature of the ideology that would fit the gestalt of contemporary activism. To start with the second part of this phrase, diversity may refer to several types of ideological ecumenism. Diversity may be about bringing together a number of different ideological perspectives into one broad movement or mobilization, and an ongoing debate revolves around the extent to which any such combination is possible or effective. Furthermore, and relatedly, the focus may also be on the ways how concerns typical of the politics of identity can be brought into a dynamic play with more traditional ideological foci such as class or capitalism. Finally, a postulate that is increasingly influential in the literature on social movements is that predominantly Western political themes and ideas should be enriched by incorporation of non-Western influences into the movements' arguments and actions – a necessity in the case of anti-neoliberal activism if it is to live up to its cosmopolitan sense of itself.

As for the first – ideational – dimension of diversity, the question is how, and to what extent, anti-neoliberal activists may benefit from the coexistence, often tense and difficult, of various ideological influences within what is often abstractly projected as one movement. James Rowe and Myles Carroll (2014, 170) put this dilemma in terms of 'dynamism' which, as they say, often occurs only 'in-itself' rather than 'for itself', namely without activists realizing that their diverse political preferences are in fact 'rooted in different tendencies'. Ideological continuities, and also endurance of internal conflicts along recognizable ideological lines, are rarely acknowledged within anti-neoliberal movements but have been noted by some scholars.[4] The point, for Rowe and Carroll (2014, 149), is that 'political differences should be openly debated' in order to contribute positively to the movement whose success depends on 'dynamism between differing wings'. Nick Dyer-Witheford's discussion (2010, 111) of the split into anarchist and socialist or social democratic movements within the politics of anti-neoliberalism follows the same vein: 'Rather than repressing this tension, or replaying it ad infinitum, it may be . . . more interesting for both sides . . . to think about the potential interplay of these two poles'. However, such ecumenical amalgamation is yet to be achieved. At this point, battles keep being fought within the anti-neoliberal space, especially between socialist and anarchist currents, usually without any reference to the ideological labels themselves (see Ibrahim 2013). At the same time, the activists' awareness of the common origin of these two political traditions and their conceptual overlaps remains hazy. Caricatures and misrepresentations abound in exchanges of diatribes regarding, on the one hand, the supposedly inevitable rigidity of the organizational straitjacket of socialism and, on the other hand, the presumed petulant pretentions of anarchists to change the world without engaging with the institutions of power. That important synergies between the two ideological perspectives are ignored is, yet again, a consequence of inadequate familiarity with past political arguments (Soborski 2013). As a matter of fact, while classical anarchists were unequivocal in their rejection of the state, it does not follow that they did not appreciate the idea of institution as a political tool. Indeed, much of classical anarchist theorizing focused on alternative institutions, be it syndicates, councils or federations (Taylor 2013, 734). In turn, with regard to socialism, its industrial and authoritarian incarnation does not exhaust what socialist tradition has to offer. The socialist conceptual reservoir also includes contributions by William Morris, Robert Owen, the Diggers and Levellers and others that cohere with the decentralized nature of anti-neoliberal move-ments. That being said, while it is compelling to suggest that the rich range of ideas available within socialism as well as anarchism could be reclaimed and reconciled for the process of forming ideological counter-hegemony, the history of anarchism's interaction with Marxism, or socialism more broadly, does not necessarily incline towards optimism as to the feasibility of such an all-inclusive project (Soborski 2007). In any case, while it makes sense to encourage activists to get to know their ideas and the history behind them – after all 'in the long run, movements that can't think can't really do too much either' (Featherstone, Henwood and Parenti n.d.) – it will be ultimately up to them to agree on the extent of common ground between their different stances.

The second dimension of diversity has to do with identitarian politics. A controversy that I noted several times in the course of this book is whether identity-related concerns rejuvenate activism or pose obstacles to effective political action. One kind of reasoning suggests that placing identity issues in the centre of activist attention leads to fragmentation of anti-neoliberal politics into particularistic mobilizations, each concerned with its own issue – race, gender, sexual orientation and so on – and hence precludes formation of an effective, overarching front of resistance. On the other hand, however, progressive politics would not deserve to be characterized as such if it were to imply a return to a world of monolithic and ascribed identities. American critical theorist and feminist Nancy Fraser elaborates on this dilemma by adapting Karl Polanyi's terminology to contemporary developments: 'Triple movement' is the concept that she uses to describe how Polanyi's 'double movement' of social protection versus marketization can be combined with the politics of emancipation:

> However much it complicates the struggle against neoliberalism, the rise of emancipation represents an advance. There is no going back to hierarchical, exclusionary, communitarian understandings of social protection, whose inno-cence has been forever shattered, and justly so. . . . We might resolve to break off our dangerous liaison with neoliberalism and forge a principled new alliance with social protection. In thereby realigning the poles of the triple movement,

we could integrate our longstanding interest in non-domination with the equally
valid interest in solidarity and social security. (Fraser 2013, 131–32)

The hope that it is possible to incorporate identity-related considerations
into counter-hegemonic politics while avoiding or at least minimizing its
fragmentation is shared by a growing number of commentators, including
this author.

Finally, in a globalizing world, genuine ideological pluralism must entail
openness to non-western perspectives. As Jackie Smith (2014, 122) writes,
'if hegemony is the exercise of intellectual and moral leadership by a dominant group, then we should look to the ways subaltern groups are shaping
discourses, values, and modes of thought'. This plea concerns relations of
domination, and ways of subverting them, both within countries and regions
and between the core and the periphery of the global system. It follows that
the effort to form an effective counter-hegemony needs to include ideological legacy of the South. It is a positive development that a degree of learning
from non-Western ideas by anti-neoliberal movements in the North is in fact
already happening. Smith (2014, 125) notes two increasingly popular indigenous discourses: 'the Rights of Mother Earth as a way of protecting both
the environment and the human rights of current and future generations [and]
buen vivir, or living well, as an alternative to perpetual growth as an orient-
ing principle for society'. These ideas 'fundamentally challenge capitalist
hegemony' and also, crucially in light of the celebration of pluralism, 'leave
room for those embracing them to imagine diverse possibilities for . . . an
alternative system' (Smith 2014, 125, 128). Expanding the ideational scope
of anti-neoliberal activism by opening it to varied cultural influences would
likely increase its appeal globally. At the same time, however, openness to
non-Western ideas should not imply a dismissal of the established ideologies
of modernity. Following Susan Buck-Morss, 'rejection of Western-centrism
does not place a taboo on using the tools of Western thought' but in fact 'frees
the critical tools of the Enlightenment . . . for original and creative application' (in Srnicek and Williams 2015, 198).

This, then, is the threefold nature of diversity that various sympathetic
commentators believe anti-neoliberal activism would do well to pursue:
diversity of ideological inputs from established traditions of political thought,
diversity of identities that should find expression within the space of activism
and cultural diversity consisting in cross-fertilization between Western and
non-Western ideas and practices. However, while anti-neoliberal movements
pledge commitment to pluralism, what is problematic about their approach
is their attempts or, more often deliberate ditching thereof, to reconcile
diversity with the need to work collectively when confronting what is a for-
midable enemy. Pluralism should be a source of strength for anti-neoliberal

movements rather than a centrifugal force undermining the pursuit of shared political goals and values. Therefore, celebration of the variety of political stances, identity considerations and cultural influences calls for a concurrent pursuit of the greatest possible synergy between them so that pluralism does not turn into Balkanization thwarting solidarity between different campaigns and mobilizations. Inevitably, this means that diversity has its limits. For example, it is not possible to reconcile progressive commitments of the anti-neoliberal left with reactionary or fascist ideas of far right challengers of neoliberalism (yet, as I noted in previous chapters, some insiders in the global justice movement advocated a left-right alliance against neoliberal hegemony as a way forward). Likewise, while activists need to be open to ideas from all over the world and sensitive to insights afforded by theories and practices of multiculturalism, this cannot entail an unlimited cultural relativism (Cohen 2009).

Ultimately, to transcend the limitations of protest politics, activism today has to stand *for* something and, to know what this something is, its respect for diversity must be balanced with a determined pursuit of unity. Following Jodi Dean, today's social movements of the left must not shy away from 'uttering the word we' (Dean 2009, 35) and imbuing it with content and meaning more concrete than the recent vague rhetoric associated with the 99 percent slogan. This is necessary in the context of an unprecedented concentration of power and resources under the control of neoliberal forces. The question is what can help bring the plethora of different mobilizations closer together and thus consolidate an effective counterbalance to neoliberalism's hegemony. Three elements spring to mind. First, an effort to identify the source of the problems that the movements struggle against is essential and, as I have argued, the very heart of radical politics. 'Anti-neoliberalism' points in the right direction but also prompts many questions: What are the origins of neoliberal hegemony and what is its nature?; where are its weak points?; what is its institutional support? and so on. Of course, to reiterate, there can be no definitive answers, but a focused deliberative process would help in sharpening the movements' understanding of the adversary and in attuning their strategies accordingly. Analysis is not something that movements can escape in favour of moralistic platitudes, or at least not without paying a potentially heavy political price. A vision of the alternative world is the second dimension. This is not to suggest the necessity of a detailed doctrine or rigid programme akin to the caricatures projected in discourses of prefigurative activism. But it is to argue that political action requires an unambiguous as well as enticing idea of what a change for the better will mean. Clichéd phrases, like 'people over profits', combined with refusal to formulate demands, meant that nothing of substance has been forthcoming from within the spaces of anti-neoliberal activism in the aftermath of the recent crisis – this needs to change if anti-neoliberal movements are to seize the next political opportunity. Finally, there is the question of how to get from here to there – namely, what strategy to pursue. Again, this is for activists themselves to consider. Yet, what seems clear is that if anti-neoliberal movements want to have any impact on the world, then they will need to actually engage with it rather than remaining in an autonomous bubble of their own making. This requires a move beyond the assumption, motivated by a particular understanding of prefigurative politics, that 'acting differently within the given socio-political structures is itself an act of profoundly altering these structures' (Rohgalf 2013, 163). In a nutshell, and this sums up the book's argument, what the movements need is an ideological vision, one open to constant revision and reinterpretation but debated overtly rather than an implicit and suppressed one which does its work behind the scenes. Whether anti-neoliberal movements have the capacity of forming a counter-hegemonic bloc or alliance will only become apparent in the process of working out shared perspectives as well as realizing where the flashpoints between any irreconcilable positions lie. Perhaps it is wishful thinking to even contemplate a united counter-hegemonic force bringing together an entire range of progressive challengers of neoliberalism. Still, it is better to know this, and hence change strategies accordingly, rather than keeping on dreaming that the world will be transformed just because activists of many different stripes have managed to camp together on behalf of the 99 percent.

All of this, of course, is easier said than done. But it seems clear that the beginning should be made by moving beyond amorphous, pre-political and narcissistic idiom of 'we are our demands' and towards a political project, however tentative, for a better society. It is important that anti-neoliberal movements get closer to a collective negotiation over this goal by initiating a serious engagement with political ideas through an inclusive but clearly focused and historically informed debate. The 'tyranny of the present' (Keane 1988, 33) inclines us to be biased in favour of a rupture with the past and against continuity. Yet, as Mark Twain is supposed to have said, history does not repeat itself, but it rhymes. It would come as a surprise to many activists today to learn how much overlap there is between the dilemmas that they face and those encountered by their forerunners in the last two centuries or so. To facilitate the formation of a counter-hegemony, anti-neoliberal activism would benefit from locating itself explicitly within a long and broad tradition of progressive political thought. This implies a clear recognition that the end ideology (or, for that matter, of history) is a hoax. The more the left withdraws from conscious ideological production the more neoliberalism advances the idea that 'there is no alternative'. The sooner anti-neoliberal movements take this onboard, the greater their chance of eventually destabilizing the neoliberal project.

NOTES

1. It is interesting that the only tangible change that Castells mentions was in fact effected through conventional political means (2015, 31–44): The post-crunch experience of Iceland is discussed by him in a separate chapter, the only one in his book to acknowledge the importance of ideological vision.

2. This is an extensive debate and one that I would not be able to adequately address in this book (even though my discussion of horizontalism and prefigurative politics is implicitly related to questions of institutional politics). Suffice it to say that some of the sharpest disagreements and disputes within anti-neoliberal camp concern the agent of political change. The alternative that is often proposed against horizontal and prefigurative modes of actions is that of political party. To justify this, critics of the anarchist or autonomist approach rely on examples drawn from recent mobilizations. For instance, the *Indignados'* abstention from any influence on the electoral contest in Spain in 2011 illustrates a possible consequence of such an anti-political approach. The movement's decision tipped the scale in favour of the conservative *Partido Popular* (PP) and against the social democratic Spanish Socialist Workers' Party (PSOE); the PP then proceeded with an outrageously unfair distribution of the costs of austerity measures thus deepening the national gap between the rich and the poor which is now one of the most extreme in Europe. On the other hand, scepticism of partisan politics that is so pervasive in anti-neoliberal circles is not without reasons as social democratic parties have failed to enact even moderately progressive agendas. In the post-crunch decade, the parties of the centre-left have proved unable or unwilling to liberate themselves from the shackles of neoliberalism and to challenge austerity in an effective way (for a detailed study of one case of the failure, see Goes 2016). Credentials of more radical, far left parties have also been shattered, if they won office, by their compliance with the global neoliberal regime as is illustrated by the Greek *Syriza* bowing to the demands of the *Troika* (Johnson 2017, 85).

3. Nick Cohen (2009, 166–67) makes a similar point: 'A paradoxical consequence of the death of the socialist idea is that Leftism now suits the consumer society very well. Because there is no coherent Left-wing political programme, anyone can affect a Leftish posture just as anyone can walk into a shop. . . . Being a Leftist is a lifestyle choice. It carries no costs and no obligations'.

4. For example, Catherine Eschle and Bice Maiguashca (2010, 174–75) identify the jagged ideological roots of the contemporary politics of global justice in the main ideologies of the left and in second-wave feminism. Heather Gautney (2010, 3, 7) stresses continuities between the discourses of 'alternative globalization' and feminism, ecologism, anarchism, socialism and communism, as well as connecting contemporary activist debates with those that raged a century ago over the impact of modernity. Mark Rupert and M. Scott Solomon (2006, 69) acknowledge the endurance of anarchism and Marxism, and 'their love-hate relationship', in the controversies dividing activists, while Mark Bray (2013) argues that the radical left, and specifically the Occupy movement, now has a predominantly anarchist nature in contrast to the domination of Marxist influences in the 1960s and 1970s. Finally, Jackie Smith and Dawn Wiest (2012, 180) view contemporary movements as 'part of an ongoing spiral of capitalism and socialism-democracy'.

Bibliography

Adam, Karla. 2011. 'Occupy Wall Street Protests Go Global'. *The Washington Post*, 15 October. Accessed 18 June 2017. https://www.washingtonpost.com/world/europe/occupy-wall-street-protests-go-global/2011/10/15/gIQAp7kimL_story.html?utm_term=.71d254d50268.

Aleya-Sghaier, Amira. 2012. 'The Tunisian Revolution: The Revolution of Dignity'. *The Journal of the Middle East and Africa* 3 (1): 18–45.

Allen, Katie and Larry Elliott. 2016. 'UK Joins Greece at Bottom of Wage Growth League'. *The Guardian*, 27 July. Accessed 6 May 2017. https://www.theguardian.com/money/2016/jul/27/uk-joins-greece-at-bottom-of-wage-growth-league-tuc-oecd.

Althusser, Louis. 2014 [1971]. *On the Reproduction of Capitalism: Ideology and Ideological State Apparatuses*. Translated by G.M. Goshgarian. London: Verso.

Amin, Ash. 2002. 'Spatialities of Globalisation'. *Environment and Planning* 34 (3): 385–99.

Anderson, Perry. 2000. 'Beyond Neoliberalism'. In *The Other Davos: The Globalization of Resistance to the World Economic System*, edited by François Houtart and François Polet. Accessed 4 March 2017. http://www.religion-online.org/blog/book-chapter/chapter-3-beyond-neoliberalism-by-perry-anderson/.

Andrejevic, Mark. 2005. 'The Work of Watching One Another: Lateral Surveillance, Risk and Governance'. *Surveillance and Society* 2: 479–97.

Andrews, Edmund L. 2008. 'Greenspan Concedes Error on Regulation'. *New York Times*, 23 October. Accessed 6 May 2017. http://www.nytimes.com/2008/10/24/business/economy/24panel.html.

Anonymous. 2012. 'Occupy: The End of the Affair'. *Social Movement Studies: Journal of Social, Cultural and Political Protest* 11 (3–4): 441–45.

Anton, Anatole. 2007. 'Socialist Voices'. In *Toward a New Socialism*, edited by Anatole Anton and Richard Schmitt, 21–52. Lanham, MD: Lexington Books.

Aron, Raymond. 2011 [1957]. *The Opium of the Intellectuals*. New Brunswick, NJ: Transaction Publishers.

Ayres, Jeffrey M. 2004. 'Framing Collective Action against Neoliberalism: The Case of the "Anti-Globalization" Movement'. *Journal of World Systems Research* 10: 2–26.

Badiou, Alain. 2012. *The Rebirth of History*. Translated by Gregory Elliott. London: Verso.

Badiou, Alain. 2013. 'Our Contemporary Impotence'. Translated by Olivia Lucca Fraser. *Radical Philosophy* 181: 43–7.

Balanyá, Belén, Brid Brennan, Olivier Hoedeman, Satoko Kishimoto and Philipp Terhorst. 2005. *Reclaiming Public Water Achievements, Struggles and Visions from around the World*. Transnational Institute and Corporate Europe Observatory.

Ball, Terence. 1997. 'Political Theory and Conceptual Change'. In *Political Theory: Tradition and Diversity*, edited by Andrew Vincent, 28–44. Cambridge: Cambridge University Press.

Barlow, John Perry. 1996. 'A Declaration of Independence of Cyberspace'. Accessed 8 July 2017. https://www.eff.org/cyberspace-independence.

Bayat, Asef. 2013. 'Revolution in Bad Times'. *New Left Review* 80: 47–60.

Beenstock, Michael. 2009. 'Market Foundations for the New Financial Architecture'. In *Verdict on the Crash: Causes and Policy Implications*, edited By Philip Booth, 59–71. London: The Institute of Economic Affairs.

Bell, Daniel. 1962. *The End of Ideology: On the Political Exhaustion of Political Ideas in the Fifties*. New York: Free Press.

Bell, Daniel. 1988. '*The End of Ideology* Revisited (Part I)'. *Government and Opposition* 23: 127–50.

Bell, Daniel. 2000. 'The Resumption of History in the New Century'. In *The End of Ideology: On the Political Exhaustion of Political Ideas in the Fifties*, xi–xxviii. Cambridge, MA: Harvard University Press.

Bennett, Lance W. 2004. 'Communicating Global Activism: Strengths and Vulnerabilities of Networked Politics'. In *Cyberprotest: New Media, Citizens and Social Movements*, edited by Wim van de Donk et al., 109–27. London: Routledge.

Bennett, Lance W. and Alexandra Segerberg. 2012. 'The Logic of Connective Action. Digital Media and the Personalization of Contentious Politics'. *Information, Communication & Society*, 15 (5): 739–68.

Berlet, Chip and Matthew N. Lyons. 2000. *Right-Wing Populism in America: Too Close for Comfort*. New York: Guilford Press.

Bey, Hakim. 2003. *T.A.Z.: The Temporary Autonomous Zone, Ontological Anarchy, Poetic Terrorism*, second edition. Brooklyn: Autonomedia.

Birch, Kean and Vlad Mykhnenko. 2010. 'Introduction: A World Turned Right Way Up'. In *The Rise and Fall of Neoliberalism: The Collapse of an Economic Order?*, edited by Kean Birch and Vlad Mykhnenko, 1–20. London: Zed Books.

Boggs, Carl. 1977/1978. 'Marxism, Prefigurative Communism, and the Problem of Workers' Control'. *Radical America* 11 (6)–12 (1): 99–122.

Boggs, Carl. 2012. *Ecology and Revolution: Global Crisis and the Political Challenge*. New York: Palgrave Macmillan.

Boltanski, Luc and Éve Chiapello. 2007. *The New Spirit of Capitalism*. Translated by Gregory Elliott. London: Verso.

Bond, Patrick and Peter McInnes. 2007. 'Decommodifying Electricity in Post-apartheid Johannesburg'. In *Contesting Neoliberalism: Urban Frontiers*, edited by Helga Leitner, Jamie Peck and Eric S. Sheppard. 157–78. London: Guilford Press.

Bookchin, Murray. 1995. *Social Anarchism or Lifestyle Anarchism*. Stirling: AK Press.

Brass, Tom. 2014. 'A Stroll in Zuccotti Park?' *Capital & Class* 38 (1): 253–57.

Bray, Mark. 2013. *Translating Anarchy: The Anarchism of Occupy Wall Street*. Winchester: Zero Books.

Breines, Wini. 1989. *Community and Organization in the New Left, 1962–1968: The Great Refusal*. New Brunswick: Rutgers University Press.

Brooke, Heather. 2012. *The Revolution Will Be Digitised*. London: Windmill Books.

Butler, Eamonn. 2008. 'Don't Knock the System: Politics Caused This Crisis of Capitalism'. Accessed 20 February 2012. https://www.adamsmith.org/blog/thinkpieces/dont-knock-the-system-politics-caused-this-crisis-of-capitalism.

Butler, Eamonn. 2009. 'The Financial Crisis: Blame Governments, Not Bankers'. In *Verdict on the Crash: Causes and Policy Implications*, edited by Philip Booth, 51–8. London: The Institute of Economic Affairs.

Butler, Judith. 2011. 'For and against Precarity'. *Tidal: Occupy Theory, Occupy Strategy* 1: 12–13. Accessed 13 August 2017. https://occupyduniya.files.word press.com/2011/12/tidal_occupytheory.pdf.

Calhoun, Craig. 2013. 'Occupy Wall Street in Perspective'. *British Journal of Sociology* 64 (1): 26–38.

Callinicos, Alex. 2010. *Bonfire of Illusions: The Twin Crises of the Liberal World*. Cambridge: Polity Press.

Callinicos, Alex and John Holloway. 2011. 'Can We Change the World without Taking Power?' (A debate at World Social Forum, Porto Alegre). Accessed 20 March 2013. https://libcom.org/library/debate-between-john-holloway-alex-call inicos-%E2%80%9Ccan-we-change-world-without-taking-power%E2%80%9D-.

Cameron, David. 2010. 'Prime Minister's Speech on the Economy', 7 June. Accessed 20 June 2017. https://www.gov.uk/government/speeches/prime-ministers-speech-on-the-economy.

Carty, Victoria. 2015. *Social Movements and New Technology*. Boulder, CO: Westview Press.

Caruso, Giuseppe. 2013. 'Justice, Equality and Conviviality: The World Social Forum's Cosmopolitan Vision'. *Interface: A journal for and about social movements* 5 (2): 78–97.

Castells, Manuel. 2010a. *The Information Age: The Rise of the Network Society*, second edition. Chichester: Wiley.

Castells, Manuel. 2010b. *The Information Age: The Power of Identity*, second edition. Chichester: Wiley.

Castells, Manuel. 2015. *Networks of Outrage and Hope: Social Movements in the Internet Age*. Cambridge: Polity Press.

Chandler, David. 2009. 'Questioning Global Political Activism'. In *What Is Radical Politics Today?*, edited by Jonathan Pugh, 77–85. London: Palgrave Macmillan.

Chossudovsky, Michel. 2016. 'The Anti-Globalization Movement and the World Social Forum. Is "Another World" Possible?' Accessed 30 July 2017. http://www .globalresearch.ca/the-anti-globalization-movement-and-the-world-social-forum-another-world-is-possible/5335181.

Christensen, Christian 2011. 'Twitter Revolutions? Addressing Social Media and Dissent'. *The Communication Review* 14 (3): 155–57.

Çiğdem. 2017. 'Turkey/Gezi'. In *Life after the Squares: Reflections on the Consequences of the Occupy Movements*, edited by Amador Fernández-Savater and Cristina Flesher Fominaya. *Social Movement Studies* 16 (1): 119–51.

Clougherty, Tom. 2009. 'How to Promote the Free Market in 2009'. Accessed 20 February 2012. https://www.adamsmith.org/blog/thinkpieces/how-to-promote-the-free-market-in-2009-2.

Cocker, Jarvis. 2012. 'Agitating for the Future'. *Big Issue*. 16 January. Accessed 16 May 2012. http://www.bigissue.com/features/458/agitating-future.

Cockett, Richard. 1995. *Thinking the Unthinkable: Think-Tanks and the Economic Counter-Revolution, 1931–1983*. London: Fontana.

Cohen, Nick. 2009. 'New Left and Old Far Right: Tolerating the Intolerable'. In *What Is Radical Politics Today?*, edited by Jonathan Pugh, 162–69. London: Palgrave Macmillan.

Cohen, Roger. 2011. 'Facebook and Arab Dignity'. *New York Times*, 24 January. Accessed 20 December 2014. http://www.nytimes.com/2011/01/25/opinion/25ihtedcohen25.html.

The Conservative Party. 2017. 'Forward, Together: Our Plan for a Stronger Britain and a Prosperous Future. The Conservative and Unionist Party Manifesto 2017'. Accessed 20 May 2017. https://www.conservatives.com/manifesto.

Conway, Janet. 2011. 'Activist Knowledges on the Anti-globalization Terrain: Transnational Feminisms at the World Social Forum'. *Interface: A journal for and about social movements* 3 (2): 33–64.

Cornell, Andrew. 2009. 'Anarchism and the Movement for a New Society: Direct Action and Prefigurative Community in the 1970s and 80s'. Institute of Anarchist Studies. Accessed 24 July 2017. http://archive.is/MYEmo.

Coser, Lewis A. 1977. *Masters of Sociological Thought: Ideas in Historical and Social Context*. New York: Harcourt Brace Jovanovich.

Crouch, Colin. 2011. *The Strange Non-Death of Neoliberalism*. Cambridge: Polity Press.

Curran, Giorel. 2006. *21st Century Dissent. Anarchism, Anti-Globalization and Environmentalism*. Houndmills, Basingstoke: Palgrave Macmillan.

Dabashi, Hamad. 2012. *The Arab Spring: The End of Postcolonialism*. London: Zed Books.

Davis, Tracy and Laura M. Harrison. 2013. *Advancing Social Justice: Tools, Pedagogies and Strategies to Transform Your Campus*. San Francisco: Jossey Bass.

Davis, William. 2016. 'The New Neoliberalism'. *New Left Review* 101: 121–34.

De Angelis, Massimo. 2000. 'Globalization, New Internationalism and the Zapatistas'. *Capital & Class* 23 (70): 9–35.

Dean, Jodi. 2009. *Democracy and Other Neoliberal Fantasies: Communicative Capitalism and Left Politics*. Durham: Duke University Press.

De la Torre, Carlos. 2016. 'Populism and the Politics of the Extraordinary in Latin America'. *Journal of Political Ideologies* 21 (2): 121–39.

Della Porta, Donatella. 2005. 'Multiple Belongings, Tolerant Identities, and the Construction of "Another Politics": Between the European Social Forum and Local Social Fora'. In *Transnational Protest and Global Activism*, edited by Donatella Della Porta and Sidney Tarrow, 175–202. Lanham, MD: Rowman & Littlefield.

Della Porta, Donatella. 2012. 'Mobilizing against the Crisis, Mobilizing for "Another Democracy": Comparing Two Global Waves of Protest'. *Interface: A journal for and about social movements* 4 (1): 274–77.

Della Porta, Donatella. 2015. *Social Movements in Times of Austerity: Bringing Capitalism Back into Protest Analysis*. Cambridge: Polity.

Dello Buono, Richard A. and José Bell Lara (eds.). 2007. *Imperialism, Neoliberalism, and Social Struggles in Latin America*. Leiden: Boston.

Desai, Radhika. 1994. 'Second-Hand Dealers in Ideas: Think-Tanks and Thatcherite Hegemony'. *New Left Review* I (203): 27–64.

Diamond, Larry. 2016. *In Search of Democracy*. London: Routledge.

Dissent! Network of Resistance against the G8 (ed.). 2005. *Shut Them Down! The G8, Gleneagles 2005 and the Movement of Movements*. Leeds: Autonomedia.

Dolata, Ulrich and Jan-Felix Schrape. 2016. 'Masses, Crowds, Communities, Movements: Collective Action in the Internet Age'. *Social Movement Studies* 15 (1): 1–18.

Dolphin, Tony and Laura Chappell. 2010. 'The Effect of the Global Financial Crisis on Emerging and Developing Economies' (Institute for Public Policy Research). Accessed 2 May 2017. http://www.ippr.org/publications/the-effect-of-the-global-financial-crisis-on-emerging-and-developing-economies.

Dutton, William H. (ed.). 2013. *The Oxford Handbook of Internet Studies*. Oxford: Oxford University Press.

Dyer-Witheford, Nick. 2010. 'Commonism'. In *What Would It Mean to Win*, edited by Turbulence Collective, 105–12. Oakland, CA: PM Press.

Earl, Jennifer, Jason Hunt, R. Kelly Garett and Aysenur Dal. 2015. 'New Technologies and Social Movements'. In *The Oxford Handbook of Social Movements*, edited by Donatella Della Porta and Mario Diani, 355–66. Oxford: Oxford University Press.

England, Kim and Kevin Ward (eds.). 2007. *Neoliberalization: States, Networks, Peoples*. Malden, MA: Blackwell.

Eschle, Catherine and Bice Maiguashca. 2010. *Making Feminist Sense of the Global Justice Movement*. Lanham, MA: Rowman & Littlefield.

Escobar, Arturo. 2009. 'Other Worlds Are Already Possible'. In *Challenging Empires: World Social Forum*, edited by Jai Sen and Peter Waterman, 393–404. Montréal: Black Rose Books.

Fadaee, Simin and Seth Schindler. 2014. 'The Occupy Movement and the Politics of Vulnerability'. *Globalizations* 11 (6): 777–91.

Featherstone, Liza, Doug Henwood and Christian Parenti. n.d. '"Action Will Be Taken": Left Anti-intellectualism and Its Discontents'. Accessed 27 July 2017. http://www.leftbusinessobserver.com/Action.html.

Fenton, Natalie and Veronica Barassi. 2011. 'Alternative Media and Social Networking Sites: The Politics of Individuation and Political Participation'. *The Communication Review* 14 (3): 179–96.

Fernández-Savater, Amador and Cristina Flesher Fominaya et al. 2017. 'Life after the Squares: Reflections on the Consequences of the Occupy Movements'. *Social Movement Studies* 16 (1): 119–51.

Filc, Dani. 2015. 'Latin American Inclusive and European Exclusionary Populism: Colonialism as an Explanation'. *Journal of Political Ideologies* 20 (3): 263–83.

The Financial Crisis Inquiry Commission. 2011. 'The Financial Crisis Inquiry Report'. Accessed 2 May 2017. https://cybercemetery.unt.edu/archive/fcic/20110310173545/http://c0182732.cdn1.cloudfiles.rackspacecloud.com/fcic_final_report_full.pdf.

Flesher Fominaya, Christina. 2014. *Social Movements and Globalization: How Protests, Occupations & Uprisings Are Changing the World*. Basingstoke: Palgrave Macmillan.

Flood, Christopher G. 2002. *Political Myth: A Theoretical Introduction*. New York: Routledge.

Frank, Thomas. 1997. *The Conquest of Cool: Business Culture, Counterculture, and the Rise of Hip Consumerism*. Chicago: The University of Chicago Press.

Franks, Benjamin. 2010. 'Anarchism and the Virtues'. In *Anarchism and Moral Philosophy*, edited by Benjamin Franks and Matthew Wilson, 135–60. Basingstoke: Palgrave Macmillan.

Fraser, Nancy. 2013. 'A Triple Movement'. *New Left Review* 81: 119–32.

Freeden, Michael. 1996. *Ideologies and Political Theory*. Oxford: Clarendon Press.

Freeden, Michael. 2003. *Ideology: A Very Short Introduction*. Oxford: Oxford University Press.

Freeman, Jo. 1972. 'The Tyranny of Structurelessness'. Accessed 10 July 2017. http://www.jofreeman.com/joreen/tyranny.htm.

Friedman, Milton. 2002 [1962]. *Capitalism and Freedom*. Chicago: University of Chicago Press.

Friedrich, Carl J. and Zbigniew K. Brzezinski. 1965. *Totalitarian Dictatorship and Autocracy*, second edition. Cambridge, MA: Harvard University Press.

Fukuyama, Francis. 1989. *Have We Reached the End of History?* Santa Monica: Rand Corporation.

Fukuyama, Francis. 1992. *The End of History and the Last Man*. London: Penguin Books.

Gamble, Andrew. 2009. *The Spectre at the Feast: Capitalist Crisis and the Politics of Recession*. Basingstoke: Palgrave Macmillan.

Ganesh, Shiv and Cynthia Stohl. 2013. 'From Wall Street to Wellington: Protests in an Era of Digital Ubiquity'. *Communication Monographs* 80 (44): 425–51.

Gaus, Gerald F. 2000. *Political Concepts and Political Theories*. Boulder: Westview Press.

Gautney, Heather. 2010. *Protest and Organization in the Alternative Globalization Era*. New York: Palgrave Macmillan.

Geertz, Clifford. 1964. 'Ideology as a Cultural System'. In *Ideology and Discontent*, edited by David Ernest Apter, 47–76. New York: Free Press of Glencoe. Accessed 25 June 2017. http://hypergeertz.jku.at/GeertzTexts/Ideology_Cultural.htm.

Gerbaudo, Paolo. 2012. *Tweets and the Streets: Social Media and Contemporary Activism*. London: Pluto Press.

Gibson, Morgan Rodgers. 2013. 'The Anarchism of the Occupy Movement'. *Australian Journal of Political Science* 48 (3): 335–48.

Giddens. Anthony. 2008. *The Third Way: The Renewal of Social Democracy*. Cambridge: Polity.

Gilbert, Jeremy. 2008. *Anticapitalism and Culture: Radical Theory and Popular Politics*. Oxford: Berg.

Gillan, Kevin and Jenny Pickerill. 2012. 'The Difficult and Hopeful Ethics of Research on, and with, Social Movements'. *Social Movement Studies* 11 (2): 133–43.

Gitlin, Todd. 1998. 'Public Sphere or Public Sphericules?' In *Media, Ritual and Identity*, edited by Tamar Liebes and James Curran, 168–75, London: Routledge.

Gladwell, Malcolm. 2010. 'Small Change: Why the Revolution Will Not Be Tweeted'. *The New Yorker*, 4 October. Accessed 2 May 2017. http://www.newyorker.com/magazine/2010/10/04/small-change-malcolm-gladwell.

Glassman, Jim. 2001. 'From Seattle (and Ubon) to Bangkok: The Scales of Resistance to Corporate Globalization'. *Environment and Planning D: Society and Space* 19: 513–33.

Goes, Eunice. 2016. *The Labour Party under Ed Miliband: Trying but Failing to Renew Social Democracy*. Manchester: Manchester University Press.

Goldman, Emma. 2005 [1924]. 'The Transvaluation of Values'. In *Anarchism: A Documentary History of Libertarian Ideas. Volume 1: From Anarchy to Anarchism (300 CE to 1939)*, edited by Robert Graham, 315–18. Montreal: Black Rose Books.

Goodwin, Barbara. 2016. *Using Political Ideas*, sixth edition. Chichester: Wiley.

Graeber, David. 2002. 'The New Anarchists'. *New Left Review* 13: 61–73.

Graeber, David. 2004. *Fragments of an Anarchist Anthropology*. Chicago: Prickly Paradigm Press.

Graeber, David. 2009. *Direct Action: An Ethnography*. Oakland, CA: AK Press.

Graeber, David. 2011. 'Occupy Wall Street Rediscovers the Radical Imagination'. *The Guardian*, 25 September. Accessed 20 February 2014. https://www.theguardian.com/commentisfree/cifamerica/2011/sep/25/occupy-wall-street-protest.

Graeber, David. 2013. *The Democracy Project: A History, a Crisis, a Movement*. New York: Spiegel and Grau.

Grande, Sandy. 2013. 'Accumulation of the Primitive: The Limits of Liberalism and the Politics of Occupy Wall Street'. *Settler Colonial Studies* 3 (3–4): 369–80.

Greenberg, Michael. 2011. 'In Zuccotti Park'. *The New York Review of Books*, 10 November. Accessed 1 August 2017. http://www.nybooks.com/articles/2011/11/10/zuccotti-park/.

Gregg, Samuel. 2009. 'Moral Failure: Borrowing, Lending and the Financial Crisis'. In *Verdict on the Crash: Causes and Policy Implications*, edited by Philip Booth, 145–53. London: The Institute of Economic Affairs.

Haldane, Andrew. 2010. 'The $100 Billion Question'. Accessed 2 May 2017. http://www.bankofengland.co.uk/archive/Documents/historicpubs/speeches/2010/speech433.pdf.

Halimi, Serge. 2017. 'We're the 99% and We're Not So United'. *Le Monde Diplomatique*, August.

Hall, Stuart. 1988. *The Hard Road to Renewal: Thatcherism and the Crisis of the Left*. London: Verso.

Halvorsen, Sam. 2012. 'Beyond the Network? Occupy London and the Global Movement'. *Social Movement Studies: Journal of Social, Cultural and Political Protest* 11 (3–4): 427–33.

Harcourt, Bernard E. 2012. 'Political Disobedience'. *Critical Inquiry* 39 (1): 33–55.

Hardt, Michael. 2002. 'Porto Alegre: Today's Bandung?' *New Left Review* 14: 112–18.

Hardt, Michael and Antonio Negri. 2000. *Empire*. Cambridge, MA: Harvard University Press.

Hardt, Michael and Antonio Negri. 2004. *Multitude: War and Democracy in the Age of Empire*. New York: Penguin.

Hardt, Michael and Antonio Negri. 2012. *Declaration*. Argo Navis.

Harris, John. 2012. 'Occupy London: What Went Wrong?' *The Guardian*, 13 February. Accessed 10 May 2017. https://www.theguardian.com/commentisfree/2012/feb/13/occupy-london-what-went-wrong.

Harvey, David. 2006. 'Neoliberalism as Creative Destruction'. *Annals of the American Academy of Political and Social Science* 610: 22–44.

Harvey, David. 2007. *A Brief History of Neoliberalism*. Oxford: Oxford University Press.

Harvey, David. 2012. *Rebel Cities: From the Right to the City to the Urban Revolution*. London: Verso.

Hayden, Tom. 2012. 'Participatory Democracy: From the Port Huron Statement to Occupy Wall Street'. *The Nation*, 16 April. Accessed 10 August 2017. https://www.thenation.com/article/participatory-democracy-port-huron-statement-occupy-wall-street/.

Hayek, Friedrich A. 1949. *The Intellectuals and Socialism*. Accessed 24 June 2017. https://mises.org/sites/default/files/Intellectuals%20and%20Socialism_4.pdf.

Heath, Joseph and Andrew Potter. 2006. *The Rebel Sell: How the Counterculture Became Consumer Culture*. Chichester: Capstone.

Hetland, Gabriel and Jeff Goodwin. 2013. 'The Strange Disappearance of Capitalism from Social Movement Studies'. In *Marxism and Social Movements*, edited by Colin Barker, Laurence Cox, John Krinsky and Alf Gunvald Nilsen, 83–102. Leiden: Brill.

Heywood, Andrew. 2017. *Political Ideologies: An Introduction*, sixth edition. London: Palgrave Macmillan.

Hickel, Jason. 2012. 'Liberalism and the Politics of Occupy Wall Street'. *Anthropology of this Century*, 4. Accessed 2 June 2017. http://aotcpress.com/articles/liberalism-politics-occupy-wall-street/.

Hindman, Matthew. 2009. *The Myth of Digital Democracy*. Princeton, NJ: Princeton University Press.

Howard, Neil and Keira Pratt-Boyden. 2013. 'Occupy London as Pre-figurative Political Action'. *Development in Practice* 23 (5–6): 729–41.

Huffington Post. 2011. '#OccupyDenver Defies National Movement, Elects "Shelby" as Official Leader'. *Huffington Post* 11 August. Accessed 11 July 2017. http://www.huffingtonpost.com/2011/11/08/occupy-denver-leader-shelby_n_1082523.html.

Huntington, Samuel. 1989. 'No Exit: The Errors of Endism'. *National Interest* 17: 3–11.

Ibrahim, Joseph. 2013. 'The Struggle for Symbolic Dominance in the British "Anti-Capitalist Movement Field"'. *Social Movement Studies: Journal of Social, Cultural and Political Protest* 12 (1): 63–80.

Iglesias, Pablo. 2015. 'Understanding Podemos'. Translated by Fruela Fernández. *New Left Review* 93: 7–22.

Inglehart, Ronald. 1971. 'The Silent Revolution in Europe: Intergenerational Change in Post-Industrial Societies'. *American Political Science Review* 65: 991–1017.

IWW. 2002 [1905]. *Preamble and Constitution*. Accessed 26 July 2017. http://www.iww.org/PDF/2002.pdf.

Jacques, Martin. 2016. 'The Death of Neoliberalism and the Crisis in Western Politics'. *The Guardian*, 21 August. Accessed 2 May 2017. https://www.theguardian.com/commentisfree/2016/aug/21/death-of-neoliberalism-crisis-in-western-politics.

Jensen, Michael J. and Henrik P. Bang. 2013. 'Occupy Wall Street: A New Political Form of Movement and Community?' *Journal of Information Technology & Politics* 10 (4): 444–61.

Johnson Pauline. 2017. 'In Search of a Leftist Democratic Imaginary: What Can Theories of Populism Tell Us?' *Journal of Political Ideologies* 22 (1): 74–91.

Jones, John. 2014. 'Compensatory Division in the Occupy Movement'. *Rhetoric Review* 33 (2): 148–64.

Jones, Owen. 2016. 'The Left Needs a New Populism Fast. It's Clear What Happens If We Fail'. *The Guardian*, 10 November. Accessed 21 August 2017. https://www.theguardian.com/commentisfree/2016/nov/10/the-left-needs-a-new-populism-fast.

Juris, Jeffrey S. 2008. *Networking Futures: The Movements against Corporate Globalization*. Durham: Duke University Press.

Juris, Jeffrey S. 2013. 'Spaces of Intentionality: Race, Class, and Horizontality at the U.S. Social Forum'. In *Insurgent Encounters: Transnational Activism, Ethnography and the Political*, edited by Jeffrey S. Juris and Alex Khasnabish, 39–65, Durham: Duke University Press.

Juris, Jeffrey S. and Alex Khasnabish. 2013. 'Ethnography and Activism within Networked Spaces of Transnational Encounter'. In *Insurgent Encounters: Transnational Activism, Ethnography and the Political*, edited by Jeffrey S. Juris and Alex Khasnabish, 1–36. Durham: Duke University Press.

Keane, John. 1988. *Democracy and Civil Society*. London: Verso.

Kessler, Jeremy K. 2011. 'The Police and the 99 Percent'. *n+1*, 10 October. Accessed 10 August 2017. https://nplusonemag.com/online-only/occupy/the-police-and-the-99-percent/.

Khasnabish, Alex. 2010. *Zapatistas: Rebellion from the Grassroots to the Global*. New York: Zed Books Ltd.

Kingfisher, Catherine. 2007. 'Spatializing Neoliberalism: Articulations, Recapitulations, and (a Very Few) Alternatives'. In *Neoliberalization: States, Networks, Peoples*, edited by Kim England and Kevin Ward, 195–222. Malden, MA: Blackwell.

Kingsnorth, Paul. 2003. *One No, Many Yeses: A Journey to the Heart of the Global Resistance Movement*. London: Free Press.

Kioupkiolis, Alexandros. 2016. 'Podemos: The Ambiguous Promises of Left-Wing Populism in Contemporary Spain'. *Journal of Political Ideologies* 21 (2): 99–120.

Klein, Naomi. 2001. 'Reclaiming the Commons'. *New Left Review* 9: 81–9.

Klein, Naomi. 2007. *The Shock Doctrine: The Rise of Disaster Capitalism*. New York: Metropolitan Books/Henry Holt.

Klein, Naomi. 2011. 'The Most Important Thing in the World'. In *This Changes Everything: Occupy Wall Street and the 99% Movement*, edited by YES! Magazine, 45–49. San Francisco: Berrett-Koehler Publishers.

Klein, Naomi. 2017. 'Now Let's Fight Back against the Politics of Fear'. *The Guardian*, 10 June. Accessed 22 June 2017. https://www.theguardian.com/books/2017/jun/10/naomi-klein-now-fight-back-against-politics-fear-shock-doctrine-trump.

Krugman, Paul. 2011. 'We Are the 99.9%'. *New York Times*, 24 November. Accessed 11 August 2017. http://www.nytimes.com/2011/11/25/opinion/we-are-the-99-9.html.

Lal, Deepak. 2009. 'The Great Crash of 2008: Are Governments or Markets to Blame?" Accessed 20 February 2012. https://www.adamsmith.org/blog/thinkpieces/the-great-crash-of-2008-are-governments-or-markets-to-blame.

Lane, Robert E. 1965. 'The Politics of Consensus in an Age of Affluence'. *The American Political Science Review* 59 (4): 874–95.

Langman, Lauren. 2013. 'Occupy: A New New Social Movement'. *Current Sociology* 61 (4): 510–24.

Langman, Lauren. 2014. 'The Carnivalization of the Public Sphere'. In *Reimagining Public Space: The Frankfurt School in the Twenty-First Century*, edited by Diana Boros and James M. Glass, 191–214. New York: Palgrave Macmillan.

Leitner, Helga, Jamie Peck and Eric S. Sheppard (eds.). 2007. *Contesting Neoliberalism: Urban Frontiers*. London: Guilford Press.

Leitner, Helga and Eric S. Sheppard. 2002. 'The City Is Dead, Long Live the Network: Harnessing Networks for a Neoliberal Era'. *Antipode* 31: 495–518.

Leitner, Helga, Eric S. Sheppard, Kristin Sziarto and Anant Maringanti. 2007. 'Contesting Urban Futures: Decentering Neoliberalism'. In *Contesting Neoliberalism: Urban Frontiers*, edited by Helga Leitner, Jamie Peck and Eric S. Sheppard, 1–25. New York: Guilford Press.

Levin, Carl and Tom Coburn. 2011. 'Wall Street and the Financial Crisis: Anatomy of a Financial Collapse' (United States Senate Permanent Subcommittee on Investigations, Committee on Homeland Security and Governmental Affairs). Accessed 2 May 2017. https://www.hsgac.senate.gov.

Leys, Colin. 1990. 'Still a Question of Hegemony'. *New Left Review* I (181): 119–28.

Libcom. 2005. 'Picket and Pot Banger Together – Class Recomposition in Argentina?' 24 July. Accessed 25 February 2012. http://libcom.org/library/argentina-aufheben-11.

Lim, Merlyna. 2012. 'Clicks, Cabs, and Coffee Houses: Social Media and Oppositional Movements in Egypt, 2004–2011'. *Journal of Communication* 62: 231–48.

Lindholm, Charles and José Pedro Zúquete. 2010. *The Struggle for the World: Liberation Movements for the 21st Century*. Stanford, CA: Stanford University Press.

Lipset, Seymour Martin. 1960. *Political Man: The Social Bases of Politics*. Garden City, NY: Doubleday and Company.

López Maya, Margarita. 2003. 'The Venezuelan Caracazo of 1989: Popular Protest and Institutional Weakness'. *Journal of Latin American Studies* 35 (1): 117–37.

Lundberg, Jacob. 2012. 'The Triumph of Global Capitalism'. Accessed 20 February 2012. https://www.adamsmith.org/blog/thinkpieces/the-triumph-of-global-capitalism.

Lyotard, Jean-François. 1984 [1979]. *The Postmodern Condition: A Report on Knowledge*. Translated by Geoff Bennington and Brian Massumi. Minneapolis: Minnesota University Press.

Ma'anit, Adam. 2007. 'A Very Social Affair'. *The Guardian*, 28 January. Accessed 30 July 2017. https://www.theguardian.com/commentisfree/2007/jan/28/socialismandsociability.

Maeckelbergh, Marianne. 2009. *The Will of the Many: How the Alterglobalisation Movement Is Changing the Face of Democracy*. London: Pluto Press.

Maeckelbergh, Marianne. 2011. 'Doing Is Believing: Prefiguration as Strategic Practice in the Alterglobalization Movement'. *Social Movement Studies: Journal of Social, Cultural and Political Protest* 10 (1): 1–20.

Maeckelbergh, Marianne. 2012. 'Horizontal Democracy Now: From Alterglobalization to Occupation'. *Interface: A journal for and about social movement* 4 (1): 207–34.

Manji, Firoze. 2007. 'World Social Forum: Just Another NGO Fair?' *Pambazuka News* 26 (288). Accessed 30 July 2017. http://www.pambazuka.org/en/category/features/39464.

Martinez-Torres, Maria Elena. 2001. 'Civil Society, the Internet, and the Zapatistas' *Peace Review* 13 (3): 347–55.

Marx, Karl and Friedrich Engels. 1970. *The German Ideology: Part One with Selections from Parts Two and Three and Supplementary Texts*, edited by C.J. Arthur. New York: International Publishers.

Marx, Leo. 2001. '*Technology*: The Emergence of a Hazardous Concept'. In *Technology and the Rest of Culture*, edited by Arien Mack, 23–46. Columbus: The Ohio State University Press.

Mason, Paul. 2012. *Why It's Kicking Off Everywhere: The New Global Revolution*. London: Verso.

Mason, Paul. 2016. *Postcapitalism: A Guide to Our Future*. London: Penguin Books.

McCurdy, Patrick, Anna Feigenbaum and Fabian Frenzel. 2016. 'Protest Camps and Repertoires of Contention'. *Social Movement Studies* 15 (1): 97–104.

McLennan, Gregor. 2009. 'Progressivism Reinvigorated'. In *What Is Radical Politics Today?*, edited by Jonathan Pugh, 145–52. London: Palgrave Macmillan.

McMahon, Sean F. 2017. *Crisis and Class War in Egypt*. London: Zed Books.

Mertes, Tom (ed.). 2004. *A Movement of Movements: Is Another World Really Possible*. New York: Verso.

Meyer, David S. 2011. 'Occupy and the Politics of Blame'. *Politic Outdoors*, 20 October. Accessed 9 August 2017. https://politicsoutdoors.com/2011/10/20/occupy-and-the-politics-of-blame/.

Milanovic, Branko. 2016. *Global Inequality: A New Approach for the Age of Globalization*. Cambridge, MA: Harvard University Press.

Minogue, Kenneth. 1994. 'Ideology after the Collapse of Communism'. In *The End of 'Isms'? Reflections on the Fate of Ideological Politics after Communism's Collapse*, edited by Alexander Shtromas. Cambridge, MA: Blackwell.

Mirowski, Philip and Dieter Plehwe (eds). 2009. *The Road from Mont Pelerin: The Making of the Neoliberal Thought Collective*. Cambridge, MA: Harvard University Press.

Moffitt, Benjamin. 2016. *The Global Rise of Populism: Performance, Political Style, and Representation*. Stanford: Stanford University Press.

Monbiot, George. 2014. 'Put a Price on Nature? We Must Stop this Neoliberal Road to Ruin'. *The Guardian*, 24 July. Accessed 17 May 2017. https://www.theguardian.com/environment/georgemonbiot/2014/jul/24/price-nature-neoliberal-capital-road-ruin.

Morozov, Evgeny. 2009a. 'The Brave New World of Slacktivism'. *Foreign Policy*, 19 May. Accessed 2 May 2017. http://foreignpolicy.com/2009/05/19/the-brave-new-world-of-slacktivism/.

Morozov, Evgeny. 2009b. 'Iran: Downside to the "Twitter Revolution"'. *Dissent* (Fall): 10–14.

Morozov, Evgeny. 2011. *The Net Delusion: How Not to Liberate the World*. London: Penguin.

Mudde, Cas. 2007. *Populist Radical Right Parties in Europe*. Cambridge: Cambridge University Press.

Mudde, Cas and Cristóbal Rovira Kaltwasser. 2011. 'Voices of the Peoples: Populism in Europe and Latin America Compared'. *Kellogg Institute Working Paper No. 378*. Notre Dame, IN: Kellogg Institute.

Mudde, Cas and Cristóbal Rovira Kaltwasser. 2013. 'Populism'. In *The Oxford Handbook of Political Ideologies*, edited by Michael Freeden, Lyman Tower Sargent, and Marc Stears, 493–512. Oxford: Oxford University Press.

Nederveen Pieterse, Jan. 2011. 'Global Rebalancing: Crisis and the East – South Turn'. *Development and Change* 42: 22–48.

Nederveen Pieterse, Jan. 2012. "Twenty-First Century Globalization: A New Development Era". *Forum for Development Studies*, 1–19.

Nik-Khan, Edward and Robert Van Horn. 2016. 'The Ascendancy of Chicago Neoliberalism'. In *The Handbook of Neoliberalism*, edited by Simon Springer, Kean Birch and Julie McLeavy, 27–38. Oxon: Routledge.

Nocera, Joe. 2012. 'Two Days in September'. *New York Times*, 14 September. Accessed 28 July 2016. http://www.nytimes.com/2012/09/15/opinion/nocera-two-days-in-september.html?smid=pl-share&_r=0.

Notes from Nowhere (ed.). 2003. *We Are Everywhere: The Irresistible Rise of Global Anticapitalism*. London: Verso.

Nunes, Rodrigo. 2005. 'Nothing Is What Democracy Looks Like; Openness, Horizontality, and the Movement of Movements'. In *Shut Them Down!*, edited by David Harvie, Keir Milburn, Ben Trott and David Watts, 299–319. Leeds and Brooklyn: Dissent! and Autonomedia.

Obama, Barack. 2009a. 'The 44th President Inauguration Speech'. *CNN*, 20 January. Accessed 22 June 2016. http://edition.cnn.com/2009/POLITICS/01/20/obama.politics/.

Obama, Barack. 2009b. 'Address in Philadelphia at the Start of the Inaugural Whistle Stop Tour', 17 January. Accessed 22 June 2016. http://www.presidency.ucsb.edu/ws/index.php?pid=85438.

O'Brien, Richard. 1992. *Global Financial Integration: The End of Geography*. London: Royal Institute of Financial Affairs.

Oldfield, Sophie and Kristian Stokke. 2007. 'Political Polemics and Local Practices of Community Organizing and Neoliberal Politics in South Africa'. In *Contesting Neoliberalism: Urban Frontiers*, edited by Helga Leitner, Jamie Peck and Eric S. Sheppard. London: Guilford Press, 139–56.

Oliver, Pamela E. and Hank Johnston. 2005. 'What a Good Idea! Ideologies and Frames in Social Movement Research'. In *Frames of Protest: Social Movements and the Framing Perspective*, edited by Hank Johnston and John A. Noakes, 185–204. Lanham: Rowman & Littlefield.

Olivera, Oscar (in collaboration with Tom Lewis). 2004. *Cochabamba! Water War in Bolivia*. Cambridge, MA: South End Press.

One-Off Press. 2001. *On Fire: The Battle of Genoa and the Anti-Capitalist Movement*. Brighton: One-Off Press.

Ostroy, Andy. 2012. 'The Failure of Occupy Wall Street'. *Huffington Post*, 31 May. Accessed 28 July 2016. http://www.huffingtonpost.com/andy-ostroy/the-failure-of-occupy-wal_b_1558787.html.

Ostry, Jonathan D., Prakash Loungani and Davide Furceri. 2016. 'Neoliberalism: Oversold?' *Finance & Development* 53 (2): 38–41. Accessed 3 May 2017. http://www.imf.org/external/pubs/ft/fandd/2016/06/ostry.htm.

Peck, Jamie. 2004. 'Geography and Public Policy: Constructions of Neoliberalism'. *Progress in Human Geography* 28: 392–405.

Peck, Jamie. 2010. *Constructions of Neoliberal Reason*. Oxford: Oxford University Press.

Peck, Jamie. 2014. 'Zombie Neoliberalism and the Ambidextrous State'. *Theoretical Criminology* 14: 104–10.

Peck, Jamie and Adam Tickell. 2007. 'Conceptualizing Neoliberalism: Thinking Thacherism'. In *Contesting Neoliberalism: Urban Frontiers*, edited by Helga Leitner, Jamie Peck and Eric S. Sheppard, 26–50. London: Guilford Press.

Pickerill, Jenny and John Krinsky. 2012. 'Why Does Occupy Matter?' *Social Movement Studies: Journal of Social, Cultural and Political Protest*, 11 (3–4): 279–87.

Piketty, Thomas. 2014. *Capital in the Twenty-First Century*. Translated by Arthur Goldhammer. Cambridge, MA: Harvard University Press.

Pleyers, Geoffrey. 2010. *Alter-Globalization: Becoming Actors in the Global Age*. Cambridge, MA: Polity Press.

Polanyi, Karl. 2001 [1944]. *The Great Transformation: The Political and Economic Origins of Our Time*. Boston: Beacon Press.

Polletta, Francesca. 2002. *Freedom Is an Endless Meeting: Democracy in American Social Movements*. Chicago: The University of Chicago Press.

Porter, Eduardo. 2014. 'Recession's True Cost Is Still Being Tallied'. *New York Times*, 22 June. Accessed 2 May 2017. https://www.nytimes.com/2014/01/22/business/economy/the-cost-of-the-financial-crisis-is-still-being-tallied.html?_r=0.

Pressebüro, Savanne. 2000. 'Right-Left – A Dangerous Flirt'. Accessed 14 July 2015. http://www.savanne.ch/right-left.en.html#fabe.

Pugh, Jonathan. 2009. 'What *Is* Radical Politics Today?' In *What Is Radical Politics Today?*, edited by Jonathan Pugh, 1–13. London: Palgrave Macmillan.

Pugh, Jonathan. 2011. 'The Stakes of Radical Politics Have Changed: Post-crisis, Relevance and the State'. In *Globalization in Crisis*, edited by Barry K. Gills, 287–99. Oxon: Routledge.

Putnam, Robert D. 2000. *Bowling Alone: The Collapse and Revival of American Community*. New York: Simon and Schuster.

Radice, Hugo. 2011 'The Prospects for Socialism: A Question of Capital and Class'. In *21st Century Socialism: Reinventing the Project*, edited by Henry Veltmeyer, 139–50. Pontypool: Merlin Press.

Rheignold, Howard. 1998. *The Virtual Community*. Accessed 8 July 2017. http://www.rheingold.com/vc/book/.

Rigon, Andrea. 2015. 'Unequal Power Relations in the Governance of the World Social Forum Process: An Analysis of the Practices of the Nairobi Forum'. *Interface: A journal for and about social movements* 7 (2): 75–97.

Rohgalf, Jan. 2013. 'Democracy of the Many? Occupy Wall Street and the Dead End of Prefiguration'. *Distinktion: Scandinavian Journal of Social Theory* 14 (2): 151–67.

Rorty, Richard. 1995. 'Movements and Campaigns'. *Dissent* (Winter): 55–60.

Rosenberg, Justin. 2005. 'Globalization Theory: A Post Mortem'. *International Politics* 42: 2–74.

Rosenhek, Zeev and Michael Shalev. 2013. 'The Political Economy of Israel's "Social Justice" Protests: A Class and Generational Analysis'. *Contemporary Social Science* 9 (1): 1–18.

Routledge, Paul and Andrew Cumbers. 2009. *Global Justice Networks: Geographies of Transnational Solidarity*. Manchester: Manchester University Press.

Rowe, James K. and Myles Carroll. 2014. 'Reform or Radicalism: Left Social Movements from the Battle of Seattle to Occupy Wall Street'. *New Political Science* 36 (2): 149–71.

Rupert, Mark. 2000. *Ideologies of Globalization: Contending Visions of a New World Order*. London: Routledge.

Rupert, Mark and M. Scott Solomon. 2006. *Globalization & International Political Economy*. Lanham, MA: Rowman & Littlefield.

Sader, Emir. 2008. 'The Weakest Link? Neoliberalism in Latin America'. *New Left Review* 52: 5–32.

Sahadi, Jeanne. 2014. 'The Top 1% and What They Pay'. *CNN Money*. Accessed 11 August 2017. http://money.cnn.com/2014/04/04/pf/taxes/top-1-taxes/.

Sakai, J. 2003. 'Aryan Politics & Fighting the W.T.O.'. In *My Enemy's Enemy. Essays of Globalization, Fascism and the Struggle against Capitalism*, edited by Anti-Fascist Forum, 7–26. Montreal: Kersplebedeb Publishing.

Sale, Kirkpatrick. 1995. *Rebels against the Future: The Luddites and Their War on the Industrial Revolution, Lessons for the Computer Age*. Basic Books.

Samuel, Henry. 2008. 'Nicolas Sarkozy Calls for Overhaul of Capitalism'. *The Telegraph*, 26 September. Accessed 22 June 2016. http://www.telegraph.co.uk/

news/worldnews/europe/france/3082611/Nicolas-Sarkozy-calls-for-overhaul-of-capitalism.html.

Santos, Boaventura de Souza. 2006. *The Rise of the Global Left: The World Social Forum and Beyond*. New York: Zed Books.

Sartori, Giovanni. 1969. 'Politics, Ideology, and Belief Systems'. *American Journal of Political Science* 63: 358–411.

Scarbrough, Elinor. 1984. *Political Ideology and Voting*. Oxford: Oxford University Press.

Scerri, Andy. 2013. 'The World Social Forum: Another World Might Be Possible'. *Social Movement Studies: Journal of Social, Cultural and Political Protest* 12 (1): 111–20.

Scholte, Jan Aart. 2005. *Globalization: A Critical Introduction*. Basingstoke: Palgrave Macmillan.

Schwarzmantel, John. 2008. *Ideology and Politics*. Los Angeles: Sage.

Scott, Alan. 1990. *Ideology and the New Social Movements*. London: Unwin Hyman.

Sen, Jai and Peter Waterman (eds). 2009. *Challenging Empires: World Social Forum*. Montréal: Black Rose Books.

Shepard, Benjamin and Roman Hayduk (eds). 2002. *From ACT UP to the WTO. Urban Protest and Community Building in the Era of Globalization*. London: Verso.

Shils, Edward. 1955. 'The End of Ideology?' *Encounter* 5: 52–58.

Shirky, Clay. 2008. *Here Comes Everybody: The Power of Organizing without Organizations*. New York: Penguin Books.

Shukaitis, Stevphen and David Graeber. 2007. 'Introduction'. In *Constituent Imagination: Militant Investigations/Collective Theorisation*, edited by Stevphen Shukaitis and David Graeber, 11–34. Oakland, CA: AK Press.

Silver, Beverly J. and Sahan Savas Karatasli. 2015. 'Historical Dynamics of Capitalism and Labor Movements'. In *The Oxford Handbook of Social Movements*, edited by Donatella Della Porta and Mario Diani, 133–45. Oxford: Oxford University Press.

Sitrin, Marina. 2006. *Horizontalism: Voices of Popular Power in Argentina*. Oakland, CA: AK Press.

Sitrin, Marina. 2011. 'Horizontalism: From Argentina to Wall Street'. *NACLA Report on the Americas*. Accessed 2 July 2017. https://nacla.org/article/horizontalism-argentina-wall-street.

Skousen, Mark. 2009. 'Has Keynes Trumped Adam Smith?' Accessed 20 February 2012. https://www.adamsmith.org/blog/thinkpieces/has-keynes-trumped-adam-smith-2.

Smith, Helen. 2016. 'A Year after the Crisis Was Declared Over, Greece Is Still Spiralling Down'. *The Guardian*, 13 August. Accessed 2 May 2017. https://www.theguardian.com/business/2016/aug/13/greek-economy-still-spiralling-down-year-after-crisis-declared-over.

Smith, Jackie. 2012. 'Connecting Social Movements and Political Moments: Bringing Movement Building Tools from Global Justice to Occupy Wall Street Activism'. *Interface: A Journal for and about social movements* 4 (2): 369–82.

Smith, Jackie. 2014. 'Counter-Hegemonic Networks and the Transformation of Global Climate Politics: Rethinking Movement-State Relations'. *Global Discourse: An Interdisciplinary Journal of Current Affairs and Applied Contemporary Thought* 4 (2–3): 120–38.

Smith, Jackie and Bob Glidden. 2012. 'Occupy Pittsburgh and the Challenges of Participatory Democracy'. *Social Movement Studies: Journal of Social, Cultural and Political Protest* 11 (3–4): 288–94.

Smith, Jackie, Michael Goodhart, Patrick Manning and John Markoff (eds). 2017. *Social Movements and World-System Transformation*. New York: Routledge.

Smith, Jackie, Marina Karides, Marc Becker, Dorval Brunelle, Christopher Chase-Dunn, Donatella della Porta, Rosalba Icaza Garza et al. 2016. *Global Democracy and the World Social Forums*. Oxon: Routledge.

Smith, Jackie and Dawn Wiest. 2012. *Social Movements in the World-System: The Politics of Crisis and Transformation*. New York: Russell Sage Foundation.

Smith, Neil. 2010. 'The Revolutionary Imperative'. *Antipode* 41 (S1): 50–65.

Soborski, Rafal. 2007. 'Is Ideological Unity against Capitalist Globalization Possible? A Conceptual Analysis'. *The International Journal of Interdisciplinary Social Sciences* 2 (3): 119–26.

Soborski, Rafal. 2009. 'Globalization: The Case for Ideological Realignment?' *Global Studies Journal* 2 (3): 87–96.

Soborski, Rafal. 2013. *Ideology in a Global Age: Continuity and Change*. Basingstoke: Palgrave Macmillan.

Soborski, Rafal. 2017. 'Ideological Imbalance Following the Credit Crunch: Neoliberalism versus the Politics of Resistance'. In *Social Movements and World-System Transformation*, edited by Jackie Smith, Michael Goodhart, Patrick Manning and John Markoff, 94–111. New York: Routledge.

Springer, Simon, Kean Birch and Julie McLeavy. 2016. *The Handbook of Neoliberalism*. Oxon: Routledge.

Srnicek, Nick and Alex Williams. 2015. *Inventing the Future: Postcapitalism and a World without Work*. London: Verso.

Stadler, Felix. 2001. 'The Space of Flows: Notes on Emergence, Characteristics and Possible Impact on Physical Space'. Accessed 2 May 2017. http://felix.openflows .com/html/space_of_flows.html.

Stanley, Ben. 2008. 'The Thin Ideology of Populism'. *Journal of Political Ideologies* 13 (1): 95–110.

Starr, Amory. n.d. 'Beyond Panic: Religious Nationalism, Political Economy, and the Blockade against Globalization'. Accessed 1 August 2017. http://trabal.org/texts/ panic.html.

Starr, Amory. 2000. *Naming the Enemy: Anti-Corporate Movements Confront Globalization*. London: Zed Books.

Starr, Amory. 2005. *Global Revolt: A Guide to the Movements against Globalization*. London: Zed Books.

Stavrakakis, Yannis and Giorgos Katsambekis. 2014. 'Left-Wing Populism in the European Periphery: The Case of SYRIZA'. *Journal of Political Ideologies* 19 (2): 119–42.

Stedman Jones, Daniel. 2012. *Masters of the Universe: Hayek, Friedman, and the Birth of Neoliberal Politics*. Princeton, NJ: Princeton University Press.

Steger, Manfred B., James Goodman and Erin K. Wilson. 2013. *Justice Globalism: Ideology, Crises, Policy*. London: Sage.

Steger, Manfred B. and Ravi K. Roy. 2010. *Neoliberalism: A Very Short Introduction*. Oxford: Oxford University Press.

Stelter, Brian. 2011. 'Camps Are Cleared, but "99 Percent" Still Occupies the Lexicon'. *New York Times*, 30 November. Accessed 9 August 2017. http://www .nytimes.com/2011/12/01/us/we-are-the-99-percent-joins-the-cultural-and-political-lexicon.html.

Stern, Chadly, Tessa V. West and Peter G. Schmitt. 2014. 'The Liberal Illusion of Uniqueness'. *Psychological Science* 25: 137–44.

Stiglitz, Joseph. 2011. 'Of the 1%, by the 1%, for the 1%'. *Vanity Fair*, 31 March. Accessed 9 August 2017. https://www.vanityfair.com/news/2011/05/top-one-percent-201105.

Szolucha, Anna. 2013. 'No Stable Ground: Living Real Democracy in Occupy'. *Interface: A journal for and about social movements* 5 (2): 18–38.

Taggart, Paul. 2004. 'Populism and Representative Politics in Contemporary Europe'. *Journal of Political Ideologies* 9 (3): 269–88.

Tarrow, Sidney. 2011. *Power in Movement: Social Movements and Contentious Politics*, third edition. Cambridge: Cambridge University Press.

Taylor, Blair. 2013. 'From Alterglobalization to Occupy Wall Street: Neoanarchism and the New Spirit of the Left'. *City: Analysis of urban trends, culture, theory, policy, action* 17 (6): 729–47.

Taylor, Dylan. 2017. *Social Movements and Democracy in the 21st Century*. Cham: Palgrave Macmillan.

Teivainen, Teivo. 2008. 'Global Civic-Driven Democratization as Political Agency'. In *Civic Driven Change: Citizen's Imagination in Action*, edited by Alan Fowler and Kees Biekart. The Hague: Institute of Social Studies. Accessed 31 July 2017. http://www.iss.nl/fileadmin/ASSETS/iss/Documents/Research_and_projects/essay-9.pdf.

The Telegraph. 2011. 'Mervyn King Is Surprised Anger at Bankers Is Not Greater'. *The Telegraph*, 1 March. Accessed 23 June 2017. http://www.telegraph.co.uk/finance/economics/8354727/Mervyn-King-is-surprised-anger-at-bankers-is-not-greater.html.

Thatcher, Margaret. 1979. *Foreword to The Conservative Manifesto*. Accessed 23 June 2017. http://www.margaretthatcher.org/document/103999.

Thompson, John B. 1990. *Ideology and Modern Culture*. Cambridge, MA: Polity Press.

Tormey, Simon. 2004. *Anti-Capitalism: A Beginner's Guide*. Oxford: Oneworld Publications.

Toynbee, Jason. 2009. 'Continuing the Struggle in Hard Times'. In *What Is Radical Politics Today?*, edited by Jonathan Pugh, 112–19. London: Palgrave Macmillan.

Tufekci, Zeynep. 2014. 'Social Movements and Governments in the Digital Age: Evaluating a Complex Landscape'. *Journal of International Affairs* 68 (1): 1–18.

Turner, Fred. 2010. *From Counterculture to Cyberculture: Stewart Brand, the Whole Earth Network and the Rise of Digital Utopianism*. Chicago: The University of Chicago Press.

Turner, Rachel S. 2008. *Neoliberal Ideology: History, Concepts and Policies*. Edinburgh: Edinburgh University Press.

UNCTAD (United Nations Conference on Trade and Development). 2016. 'Trade and Development Report'. Accessed 1 June 2017. http://unctad.org/en/PublicationsLibrary/tdr2016_en.pdf.

Van Gelder, Sarah. 2011. 'How Occupy Wall Street Changes Everything'. In *This Changes Everything: Occupy Wall Street and the 99% Movement*, edited by YES! Magazine, 1–12. San Francisco: Berrett-Koehler Publishers.

Van Laer, Jeroen. 2010. 'Activists Online and Offline: The Internet as an Information Channel for Protest Demonstrations'. *Mobilization* 15 (3): 347–66.

Vestergren, Sara, John Drury and Eva Hammar Chiriac. 2017. 'The Biographical Consequences of Protest and Activism: A Systematic Review and a New Typology'. *Social Movement Studies* (16) 2: 203–21.

Wallerstein, Immanuel. 2011. 'The Fantastic Success of Occupy Wall Street Commentary', 15 October. Accessed 13 February 2017. http://www.iwallerstein.com/fantastic-success-occupy-wall-street/.

Ward, Kevin and Kim England. 2007. 'Conclusion: Reflections on Neoliberalizations'. In *Neoliberalization: States, Networks, Peoples*, edited by Kim England and Kevin Ward, 248–62. Malden, MA: Blackwell.

The Washington Times. 2011. 'Editorial: From Arab Spring to Islamist Winter'. *The Washington Times*, October 25. Accessed 16 May 2017. http://www.washingtontimes.com/news/2011/oct/25/from-arab-spring-to-islamist-winter/

Webster, Sean. 2011. 'Has social media revolutionized revolutions?' *World News*, February 16. Accessed 20 December 2014. http://www.jcunews.com/2011/02/16/has-social-media-revolutionized-revolutions.

Welty, Emily E. 2014. 'Occupy Wall Street as "American Spring"?' *Peace Review: A Journal of Social Justice* 26 (1): 38–45.

Whitaker, Chico. 2009. 'The World Social Forum As Open Space'. In *Challenging Empires: World Social Forum*, edited by Jai Sen and Peter Waterman, 81–93. Montréal: Black Rose Books.

Winlow, Simon, Steve Hall, James Treadwell and Daniel Briggs. 2015. *Riots and Political Protest: Notes from the Post-Political Present*. Oxon: Routledge.

Wolfson, Todd and Peter Funke. 2017. 'Contemporary Social Movements and Media: The Emergent Nomadic Political Logic and Its Nervous System'. In *Social Movements and World-System Transformation*, edited by Jackie Smith, Michael Goodhart, Patrick Manning and John Markoff, 76–93. New York: Routledge.

Wright, John S.F. 2015. 'The Pathway Out of Neoliberalism and the Analysis of Political Ideology in the Post-Crisis World'. *Journal of Political Ideologies* 20 (2): 109–33.

WSF. 2001. 'World Social Forum Charter of Principles'. In *Challenging Empires: World Social Forum*, edited by Jai Sen and Peter Waterman, 69–71. Montréal: Black Rose Books.

Wylde, Christopher. 2012. *Latin America after Neoliberalism: Developmental Regimes in Post-Crisis States*. London: Palgrave Macmillan.

Zinn, Howard. 2015. *A People's History of the United States: 1492 – Present*, third edition. London: Routledge.

Žižek, Slavoj. 2011. 'Shoplifters of the World Unite'. *London Review of Books*, 19 August. Accessed 1 August 2016. http://www.lrb.co.uk/2011/08/19/slavoj-zizek/shoplifters-of-the-world-unite.

Žižek, Slavoj. 2013. 'The Simple Courage of Decision: A Leftist Tribute to Thatcher'. *New Statesman*, 17 April. Accessed 20 February 2014. http://www.newstatesman.com/politics/politics/2013/04/simple-courage-decision-leftist-tribute-thatcher.

Zuckerberg, Mark. 2012. 'Letter from Mark Zuckerberg'. Accessed 14 July 2017. https://www.sec.gov/Archives/edgar/data/1326801/000119312512034517/d287954ds1.htm#toc287954_10.

Zürn, Michael and Pieter de Wilde. 2016. 'Debating Globalization: Cosmopolitanism and Communitarianism as Political Ideologies'. *Journal of Political Ideologies* 21 (3): 280–301.

Index

About the Author

Rafal Soborski is Professor of International Politics at Richmond, the American International University in London. He has published extensively on globalization, ideology, Euroscepticism and green political thought. His previous book is *Ideology in a Global Age*: *Continuity and Change* (Palgrave Macmillan 2013). He is the editor of *The Global Studies Journal*.